THE BEST TIME TO ACT

The Best Time to Act

Classic sketches and new material from the Riding Lights repertoire

Paul Burbridge and Murray Watts

Hodder & Stoughton

LONDON SYDNEY AUCKLAND

British Library Cataloguing in Publication Data
A record for this book is available from the British Library

ISBN 0 340 62144 3

Cover photo: Robert Duncan in Rolling in the Aisles
By: Robin Hart

Typeset by Hewer Text Composition Services, Edinburgh
Printed and bound in Great Britain by
Cox & Wyman Ltd, Reading, Berkshire

Hodder and Stoughton
A division of Hodder Headline PLC
338 Euston Road
London NW1 3BH

For Tony Collins
friend and original publisher,
without whose relentless and
unbalanced enthusiasm
the public would largely have been
spared books such as this

I hear, I forget.
I see, I remember.
I do, I understand.
ANCIENT PROVERB

LICENCE TO PERFORM THE SKETCHES IN THIS BOOK

Please read this information carefully, even if you think you may already have permission to perform sketches from this volume.

Any performance of a sketch in this book must be given under licence. This is in accordance with the normal procedure relating to published theatrical work. Instead of granting permission for each performance of a single sketch, we have decided to continue the policy, established in our previous books, of issuing a licence covering all the material in *The Best Time to Act* for a fixed fee.

However, much, though not all, of the material in this compilation has been published previously in *Time to Act*, *Lightning Sketches* and *Red Letter Days*. Licences have been issued relating to these books, so it is important to establish the appropriate licensing category relevant to you or to your group. You may be entitled to a reduction of the fee.

Category One

(*for those who do not hold any current licences*)
A performing licence for the material in *The Best Time to Act* costs **£25.00**, renewable after five years.

Category Two

(*for those who hold a current performing licence for* **one** *of the following books: Time to Act, Lightning Sketches, Red Letter Days*)
When making your application, please quote the reference number and name of licensee from your original licence.

You will then benefit from a reduction. Your new performing licence for *The Best Time to Act* will cost **£15.00**.

Category Three

(*for those who hold* **two** *or* **three** *current licences, relating to Time to Act, Lightning Sketches or Red Letter Days*)
When making your application, please quote the titles, reference numbers and names of the licensees on the licences you already hold. You will then benefit from a reduction. Your new licence for *The Best Time to Act* will cost **£5.00**.

Please check that your licences are still valid. A licence for *Lightning Sketches* is valid for three years; a licence for *Red Letter Days* is valid for five years; a licence for *Time to Act* is valid for life.

The following conditions apply to all licences:

1 The licence will be issued in the name of the individual or group intending to perform the sketches. Licences are not transferable.
2 It guarantees the right to perform all the sketches for a period of **five years**, as often as the licensee wishes. (We cannot make exceptions for 'one-off' performances of an individual sketch but hope that the purchase of a licence will encourage fuller use of the material.) The licence is renewable after five years.
3 It does not confer the right to reproduce the text in any form. (See the copyright note.) Acknowledgements at any performance should mention the title of the book, authors and publishers, in writing if possible.
4 All cassette recording, radio, television, video and film rights are reserved.

All licence applications should be sent to: **'The Best Time to Act', P.O. Box 223, York YO1 1GW.**

All cheques and money orders should be made out in pounds sterling and made payable to 'The Best Time to Act'.

NB The above refers to amateur productions (to paying and non-paying audiences). Professional companies wishing to perform this material should make a separate application to the same address, describing the details of their intended production. Permission will involve payment of royalties on box-office receipts.

CONTENTS

Contents

INTRODUCTION

Sixteen years ago, almost to the day, we nervously penned the introduction to the original *Time to Act*. A little while later our publishers, rather more nervously, received the manuscript. They were taking a very serious risk with us. The book was unclassifiable and, as far as the readership was concerned, completely without precedent. A book of short dramatisations of biblical stories? Well, okay so far, this was not unknown – but mainly *comic* sketches? Dangerously close to the edge, but even this was just about possible without bringing the imprint of 'Hodder Religious Books' into total disrepute. However, guest appearances of Dracula in 'The Parable of the Talents'? Football hooligans, upper-class twits, social workers, city executives, smooth-talking salesmen, cowboys, vicars chanting plainsong in the toilets of an InterCity train?? 'The Parable of the *Good Punk Rocker*'??? It was clearly insane to publish. Luckily, however, at least one of the editors at Hodder was insane, and this splendid tradition among the staff at Religious Books has continued ever since.

Over the last sixteen years, *Time to Act*, which many thought would break records for the extreme brevity of its shelf life, has been continuously in print. It has gone through many impressions in English, and has been translated into French, Swedish, Norwegian and Welsh, not to mention individual sketches being performed in Zulu, Auca Indian, Pidgin New Guinea, Punjabi and, by far the most challenging, Scouse. *Time to Act* was soon followed by *Lightning Sketches* and *Red Letter Days*, and this book – which supersedes all three – is an anthology of the best of all the books, with new material of its own. We hope that *The Best Time to Act* is not simply the climax of an adventure over the last two decades,

but an encouragement to all our readers and performers for
the next decade.

The first sketches ever performed by the infant Riding
Lights Theatre Company, in 1977, were 'The Light of the
World' and 'The Parable of the Good Punk Rocker'. Our
'world premiere' was in a little church in Bradford. Years
later, the company visited India and were invited to a
theatre performance by Indian students. The two pieces
they performed to us were 'The Light of the World' and
'The Parable of the Good Punk Rocker'. It is hard to convey
the depth of our feeling, the humbling experience of our work
being offered back to us, changed and enriched, from across
the other side of the world. And, invariably, it is these two
sketches more than any others that seem to have become
associated with *Time to Act* as it has travelled through barriers
of language and culture: 'The Good Punk Rocker' is wild,
zany, a burst of energy celebrating the message 'love your
neighbour'; 'The Light of the World' is serious, a meditation
on the cross and the meaning of divine love. It is fitting that
these two profound aspects of the gospel – expressed in
the poverty and simplicity of obscure community theatre –
should be our most popular works. They originated, even
before Riding Lights, in our first street theatre project in
North Wales. They were first performed in a pub car park
in Abersoch.

This summer, one of the authors was on a boat travelling
to Albania, attempting an extreme form of escapism from
drama, script deadlines, Riding Lights, the BBC, only to find
himself in conversation with a passenger who – it turned out
– had performed 'The Good Punk Rocker' in her youth club.
Is there no escape from the ubiquity of this sketch? And will
we have to answer for this at the Last Judgement? 'Authors of
"The Parable of the Good Punk Rocker" . . . hmmn . . . that
tiresome piece of rubbish which we've been forced to watch
year after year, one zealous church group after another!!'
'But – but – ' 'Second on the left, down the long chute.'
'But we were only trying to make the gospel relevant to
the modern a-aaaaaaaaaargh . . .'

Yet discussions about 'The Good Punk Rocker' in Albania

are not as crazy as they sound. So much has happened since *Time to Act* was published sixteen years ago. One of the early full-length plays performed by Riding Lights was based on the diary of a Christian, incarcerated in a Soviet mental hospital because of 'dissident' beliefs. Now the founders of Riding Lights are involved, through S4C and the BBC, in a major co-production with Moscow studios to produce an animated version of the Bible, for a world-wide audience of many millions. It is inconceivable that we, at least, would have been part of these exciting developments had it not been for the pilgrimage which began with the simple retelling of biblical stories in *Time to Act*. The world has changed, but the need to re-examine, to explore, and to thrill audiences with both the funny and the serious sides to faith has not changed. If anything, it has become much more urgent in a civilisation which is drifting towards loss of meaning; where, as C.S. Lewis remarked, the danger of abandoning Christianity is not so much that people will believe nothing, but that they will believe anything. This is now a peril for both East and West. We are moving into an age of gullibility and superstition, and the widespread exploitation of the young and vulnerable.

When *Time to Act* first appeared, many of our new generation of readers and actors had not been born. The challenges they now face are considerable but there is still a huge potential for contributing, however humbly, to the enrichment of our society and our culture. This is truly the *best* time to act. So under this title we are launching our anthology, including the favourite and most useful sketches from our three books with Hodder, as well as a few articles which we consider to be important. But we have also added a number of new sketches, some of them from the award-winning comic revues of Riding Lights at the Edinburgh Festival. They are included simply for fun. And if that is all we offer to many of our readers, we will be quite happy – because laughter is one of the richest gifts. Where there is laughter in the world, as Riding Lights has experienced with amazement and joy even in the most desperately troubled places (Belfast in the late seventies, Soweto in the early eighties), there is often the brightest flame of hope burning. A hope that can transform the world.

'The light shines in the darkness' is the key phrase of our sketch, 'The Light of the World'. The best phrases, and certainly the enduring ones, come from the Bible. As does the phrase, 'Time to act'. 'It is time for the Lord to act' (Ps. 119:126). Ultimately, the emphasis is not on what we must do, but on what he has done and will do. Our twentieth-century 'gloss', the jokes, the off-beat humour, even the serious moments, are like Christmas wrapping paper which is chosen to attract and then to be discarded in favour of something more precious; or like the poor swaddling clothes around the Christ-child in the old stable, a rough and temporary context for the truth. We hope there is a light that shines through all earthly limitations, a light which celebrates our humanity, our frailty and our absurdity. For there is One who accepts us as we are and loves us.

Our hopes, expressed in our first introduction in 1978, have not changed but deepened:

> The kingdom of God is not easily confined to our systems, whether artistic, theological, or materialistic, and it is certainly not possible to encapsulate the greatness of God in a sketch. What it is possible to do is to direct attention, humbly but confidently, to a God who communicates:
>
> > The Mighty One, God the Lord,
> > speaks and summons the Earth
> > from the rising of the sun to its setting.
> > Out of Zion, the perfection of beauty,
> > God shines forth. (Ps. 50)
>
> The wonder of it is that God chooses people to communicate his character and that he does not despise the limitations of our personalities. He does not crush us and mould us into conveyor-belt Christians, but he adorns our lives with laughter, compassion, individuality and different gifts. Therefore, though we know that this book

is really conditioned by our personalities, we also believe that God has condescended to communicate something of himself through us and, potentially, through any of our readers.

Paul Burbridge and Murray Watts
YORK
NOVEMBER, 1994

Angel Space

RAPHAEL, *an Archangel*; HERION, *an angel*

Despite its simplicity, this sketch is quite difficult to perform well. There is little action, so the challenge to the actors is in allowing the vividness of the language to stimulate the imagination of the audience. Many people have an understandably vague conception of supernatural beings, therefore strong characterisation is important. RAPHAEL *could be somewhat avuncular, for instance* HERION, *wide-eyed and enthusiastic. Perhaps because of its mixture of gentleness, humour and poignancy, this sketch has become one of the most well-loved in this book. It makes the Christmas theme appropriate at any time in the year.*

Angel costumes can often provoke unnecessary amusement, so unless something simple and *dignified can be found (preferably without wings), the hazard is best avoided altogether in favour of stylised modern dress. One style which Riding Lights has used was created by red boiler-suits, hard hats and clerical collars.*

RAPHAEL *is discovered on stage. After a pause,* HERION *enters and without seeing* RAPHAEL *comes downstage, looking around above the audience, at first cautiously, then with an increasing sense of wonder.*

RAPHAEL: What brings *you* to the gates of Heaven, angel?
HERION: (*Surprised at being discovered*) Oh . . . um . . . nothing.
RAPHAEL: Nothing?
HERION: No, I just came outside to look. I'm sorry, I'll go back.
RAPHAEL: Have you never been outside before?
HERION: No. (*Ruefully*) I'm only a minor cherub. I haven't

been given my wings yet. But one day soon I hope to fly
swiftly at my Master's bidding – like the others.

RAPHAEL: What is your name?

HERION: Herion. What's yours?

RAPHAEL: Raphael.

HERION: (*Gulp*) Oh, I've never spoken to an Archangel
before.

RAPHAEL: What were you looking for?

HERION: Nothing in particular. I've just heard so much about
the wonder of all created things, so I wanted to see for
myself. I'm not restless or anything, but I meet so many
angels returning from flight far and wide in the universe,
their eyes almost popping out of their heads as they try to
describe what they've seen.

RAPHAEL: I know the feeling. Even when you fly faster than
light, you never seem to come anywhere near the end.

HERION: I wish I could go.

RAPHAEL: Well, soon maybe. But you can see quite a lot
from where we're standing. I'll show you. (*He comes
downstage and gestures upwards, as if throwing back a
huge curtain*)

HERION: It's bigger than I could have possibly imagined.

RAPHAEL: It's bigger than you could possibly see. Eternal
motion of stars and galaxies. Old ones die and grow cold;
new ones burn blue and white like those up there.

HERION: Millions of them. As if a paintbrush, full of light,
has been flicked across the sky again and again.

RAPHAEL: And each gap between the stars is a window
into distant space beyond. Star after star, their messages still travelling long after they themselves have
gone out.

HERION: Oh, wow! (*Pause*) Do Archangels ever feel small?

RAPHAEL: All the time.

HERION: Wouldn't it be great if we could all go on a guided
tour of the universe? You could show us round.

RAPHAEL: A lot of us did go out together once . . . when
the Son of Almighty God himself left the splendour of
Heaven and went to live on earth for a while. It was a
pretty important occasion, so we took the choir along.

Filled the sky with singing, just to let them know he'd arrived.

HERION: The people on earth must have loved that.

RAPHAEL: Oh, yes. Made them jump, too.

HERION: Earth must be a fabulous place for the Son of God to go and live there. Is it like Heaven?

RAPHAEL: It used to be, before it was spoilt.

HERION: I bet it's that great big orange planet up there, 'cos it *is* going a bit pink at the edges, isn't it?

RAPHAEL: No, not that one. You can hardly see it, actually. It's that little dim one down there.

HERION: (*Peering into outer space*) You can't be serious?

RAPHAEL: I am.

HERION: It looks like a chewed-up golf-ball. What in Heaven did he want to go down there for?

RAPHAEL: To help them. To put right what was spoilt.

HERION: Did he rule the earth then?

RAPHAEL: Not in the same way as he now rules with God in Heaven.

HERION: But how did he live? Did you all go and build him a palace, or something?

RAPHAEL: He was born in a cattleshed, and lived in various places, wandering . . .

HERION: Born??

RAPHAEL: Yes. As a man.

HERION: You mean he changed into . . . something else?

RAPHAEL: He became very small. Nothing more than a seed – and was born on to the earth.

HERION: How horrible.

RAPHAEL: It was the only way – to help them. But surely you've learnt that about God by now. You spoke of the wonder of all created things: the real wonder is that God cares for each one of them (*Pointing to earth*) that much.

HERION: It's a wonder to me that he didn't come to grief down there on that miserable place.

RAPHAEL: Well, he did . . . and he didn't. But there was a happy ending, as you know.

HERION: Tell me about it.

RAPHAEL: I would if I had time, but 'E'en Eternity's too short' and all that. I must fly. But stay here and watch if you like. (*He exits, leaving* HERION *studying the sky as the lights fade*)

What to do on a Rainy Day

NARRATOR ONE; NARRATOR TWO; NOAH'S ELDER BROTHER; NOAH; SHEM, *his eldest son*; HAM, *his dullest son*; JAPHETH, *his youngest son*; DEREK, *a rare species*; OTHER ACTORS IN THE MIME; GOD.

The format of two narrators presenting a story illustrated by mime has been tried and tested often enough. Here, the style has been developed to give much more of the dialogue to the characters themselves, but the narrated sequences should still be accompanied by simple and imaginative action. Much of this has been left for you to stage. All props and costumes should emphasise the cartoon element of the presentation.

Admittedly, this is a somewhat 'baroque' treatment of one of the best-loved stories in the Bible and for this reason the director may wish to prune some of the more whimsical scenes for the sake of a more straightforward authenticity. However, if you have the time (and the courage) you will find here an epic to suit an epic.

ONE: The story of Noah. (*Ancient actor shakily makes his way on to the stage*)

TWO: Noah was a remarkable man.

ONE: He was six hundred and fifty years old. (*Still making his way across the stage, the ancient actor dies suddenly*)

TWO: Ah. Never mind.

ONE: He had to go sometime.

TWO: Thank you very much. (*Actor leaves*)

ONE: However, Noah had a brother.

TWO: Also called Noah.

ONE: Who was only six hundred years old.

TWO: He was the one mentioned in Genesis, chapter six. (*Enter Noah carrying a placard saying, 'Prepare to meet thy God'*)

ONE: Noah was a blunt man.

TWO: He was dropped as a baby.

ONE: Noah was the least successful preacher in the history of the world.

TWO: But he was very good with animals.

ONE: As a preacher his message was a failure.

TWO: But his techniques were imaginative.

ONE: He turned up to fancy-dress parties.

TWO: Dressed as a coffin. He turned up at beach parties.

ONE: Selling umbrellas.

TWO: The crowds flocked to avoid him speaking.

ONE: Noah had reached the end of himself.

TWO: This was it.

ONE: He had failed.

TWO: Totally.

ONE: Utterly.

TWO: Completely.

ONE: But . . .

TWO: He was still . . .

TOGETHER: Very good with animals!

TWO: And God said:

GOD: Noah, I've heard you're good with animals.

ONE: And Noah said:

NOAH: Yea, Lord, I am also keen on wild flowers, but mine earnest desire is to be an preacher of thy righteous word.

TWO: And God said:

GOD: Fair enough, Noah, I have seen your righteousness.

NOAH: Yet, O Lord, it troubleth me exceeding great that my preaching of thy word doth fall on stony ground.

GOD: Let me explain, Noah.

NOAH: Speak, Lord, for thy servant is all ears.

GOD: The first problem is your quirky use of the Authorised Version, which is highly alienating to the modern culture.

ONE: And Noah said:

NOAH: Fair enough, Lord. I picked it up in prayer meetings.

TWO: But God said:

GOD: However, that is nothing compared with the violence and corruption that have hardened men's hearts. Now listen carefully.

NOAH: Yea, er, yes, Lord.

GOD: I have lost patience with the wickedness of mankind. I have decided to destroy all the human race. (NOAH *looks crestfallen*) Except . . . you and your family. (NOAH *cheers up*) For you are the only ones on the Earth who serve me.

NOAH: Lord, you have really encouraged me by saying that.

ONE: And God said:

GOD: To be safe, you'll have to build yourself a boat.

NOAH: Right, Lord, a boat.

GOD: A very large boat.

NOAH: Large boat, yup. (*Making notes*)

GOD: In the middle of the desert.

NOAH: (*Writing*) In the middle of the . . . desert. (*He hesitates*) Um, why would that be, Lord?

GOD: Because that's the only way that you and your family can be saved.

NOAH: Aha. I see! (*He obviously doesn't*) Shall I consult my psychiatrist now, or after I've built the boat in the middle of the desert?

GOD: Noah, I am going to cause a mighty flood to cover the whole Earth as judgement for man's wickedness.

NOAH: Ah! Flood, desert, boat, float. Yes, I see it all!

GOD: Well, would you go and do it all.

NOAH: Right, Lord.

TWO: God told Noah to build himself an ark.

HAM: (*Entering with a small painted rainbow*) Hey, I've got an arc!

ONE: Not that sort of arc.

HAM: Oh, sorry. Is this for later on?

TWO: Yes, that's the wrong prop. That comes at the end.

HAM: Fine. (*He turns to leave*) I'll keep it out then, shall I?

ONE: (*Losing patience*) Yes! (*Recovering*) So God told Noah to build himself an –

HAM: (*Shouting from offstage*) I'm putting it on the table.

ONE: AN ARK!

TWO: So Noah set to work with his three sons,

ONE: Shem, (*Enter* SHEM)

TWO: Ham (*Enter* HAM)

ONE: And Japheth. (*Enter* JAPHETH)

TWO: Who wath the youngetht.

ONE: Thank you.

TWO: Noah got the plans from God.

ONE: It was to be built of gopher wood.

NOAH: (*Making further notes*) Gopher wood. (HAM *rushes offstage and returns with a small piece of wood*)

HAM: Here you are.

NOAH: What's this?

HAM: It's pine.

NOAH: I said gopher wood.

HAM: I did.

NOAH: (*Exasperated*) GOPHER! *Gopher* wood! (HAM *still looks confused*) Oh, never mind. You make the tea.

ONE: So Ham, Shem and Japheth got on with the building. (*Music – e.g. 'The Sailor's Hornpipe'. There is a period of intense activity. The three lads work with a will, while* NOAH *peers into his notebook and orders everyone about*)

TWO: Noah did the calculations,

ONE: Shem planed the planks,

TWO: Japheth jigged the joists

ONE: And Ham hammered the nails. (*They stand back to survey their work*)

TWO: Together they built themselves a tall, thin structure, not unlike a telegraph pole.

ONE: So . . . (*More frantic activity*)

TWO: Shem deplaned the planks,

ONE: Japheth rejigged the joists,

TWO: Ham unhammered the nails,

ONE: And Noah was taken off the calculations altogether.

ALL: But he was very good with animals! (SHEM, HAM *and* JAPHETH *continue to build the ark.* NOAH *comes downstage to talk to* GOD)

TWO: And talking of animals,

ONE: God said to Noah:

GOD: Hey, Noah, you're good with animals. Round up two of every species, animals, birds and creeping things, clean and unclean, every kind of creature and bring them into the ark.

TWO: And Noah said:

NOAH: Lord, I think you may have forgotten something. The fish. (*Pause*) But on the other hand, thinking about it, *I* may have forgotten something which is the fact that fish can swim . . . and they may in fact quite enjoy the whole . . . um . . . experience. So, fine. Yup. I see it all.

ONE: And God said:

GOD: Well, would you just go and do it all.

NOAH: Right, Lord. I'll be hurrying along then. (*Exit* NOAH, *changing his placard to 'Prepare to meet thy Dog'*) Here, boy! (*Whistling*) Come to Noah. Come on. (*His voice fades out offstage*)

ONE: Meanwhile, back at the ark,

TWO: The building continued.

ONE: The whole ark was waterproofed with boiling pitch.

TWO: Shem held up the brush,

ONE: Japheth held up the ladder

TWO: And Ham held up the progress.

ONE: But in spite of this,

TWO: The ark was finished

ONE: And Noah returned

TWO: Having completed his mighty work of conservation. (*He enters*)

NOAH: Save the tiger!

SHEM: Save the badger!

JAPHETH: Save the whale!

HAM: We'll have it tomorrow with a salad.

ONE: Look, I'm warning you.

HAM: Sorry.

TWO: Noah had collected all the animals.

ONE: The birds of the air,

TWO: The beasts of the field

ONE: And every creeping thing that creeps upon the Earth.

ACTOR: (*Gushing*) Oooh, Noah, what a *wonderful* ark! Did you make it all yourself?

NOAH: (*Harshly*) Get in!

ONE: Every creature entered the ark.

TWO: The big ones,

ONE: Two by two by two;

TWO: The little ones,

ONE: Two by two by two;

TWO: The tiny ones,

ONE: Two by two by two;

TWO: The tiny weeny ones (HAM *rushes on, accidentally squashing a small but significant species of beetle*)

ONE: Two by two by – splat!

HAM: Whoops. Sorry.

TWO: Here's the net.

ONE: (*Hands it to* HAM) Off you go.

HAM: (*Singing*) The animals went in one by one, one by one . . .

TWO: Get out.

HAM: Sorry. (*Exit*)

ONE: So, finally,

TWO: When they were all in,

ONE: Checked

TWO: And double-checked,

ONE: Stabled,

TWO: Kennelled

ONE: And perched,

TWO: Noah shut the great gopher-wood door. (*Enter* DEREK, *out of breath. His costume is a bizarre mixture of horse and drying rack. Various items of clean underwear are attached to his outstretched arms. These remain hidden inside his coat*)

DEREK: Hey, wait for me!

NOAH: (*Wearily*) Who are you?

DEREK: I'm a rare species.

NOAH: (*Consulting his inventory*) What are you called?

DEREK: Derek.

NOAH: No, what's the species called?

DEREK: I'm a kind of horse.

NOAH: Sorry. We've got horses.

DEREK: (*Revealing the line of washing*) Not a clothes-horse.

NOAH: Look, we've got a full quota of clean and unclean animals. Which are you?

DEREK: Well, most of these are clean, except for the socks.

NOAH: Have you got a mate?

DEREK: Nope.

NOAH: We only have two of everything on here.

DEREK: You could always cross me with something. Cross these with your pandas and you'd get a pair of underpandas.

NOAH: Very funny.

DEREK: Well, I just thought I'd air it with you.

NOAH: Sorry, you can't come in with jokes like that.

DEREK: Oh, go on. I've just tumble-dried all these.

NOAH: Oh, all right.

ONE: And the door was finally shut.

TWO: Outside, crowds of people in sunglasses,

ONE: Sipping lemonade,

TWO: Mocked and jeered

ONE: Until . . .

TWO: Rumble, rumble.

ONE: Storm clouds approached,

TWO: The sky darkened,

ONE: The horizon vanished,

TWO: Torrential rain lashed the desert.

ONE: Empty riverbeds were engulfed in foaming waters

TWO: And the sale of choc ices fell off.

ONE: Splat!

TWO: Thank you.

ONE: And the people cried out to Noah:

ACTOR 1: (*'Burbling' his lips with his hand*) Hey! Noah! Any chance of a late booking?

ACTOR 2: (*Also burbling*) I believe! I believe . . . I believe that I'm drowning!

ACTOR 3: (*Burbling*) May God bless her, and all who sail in her!

TWO: But the door was shut.

ONE: And the ark rose high above the land.

TWO: For forty days

ONE: And forty nights

TWO: It was carried on the waters of the flood.

ONE: Inside the ark

TWO: It was cosy,

ONE: It was dry,

TWO: It was warm.

ONE: (*Holding nose*) Too warm.

TWO: It was extremely close

ONE: And Noah opened all the portholes

TWO: And noticed that the rain had stopped.

ONE: He let out a great whoop,

TWO: But it couldn't swim,

ONE: So he tried a raven.

TWO: That couldn't swim either,

ONE: But it could fly,

TWO: And it flew back and forth across the water

ONE: Looking for dry land.

TWO: After several more attempts with various birds,

ONE: Noah tried a chicken,

TWO: Which was absolutely delicious.

ONE: His last attempt was a dove,

TWO: Which returned to the ark carrying an olive branch.

ONE: He knew that the waters had abated.

TWO: He called to his family:

NOAH: (*In the immortal style of Long John Silver*) HAHA-
HAHAHAHA! Shem lad! Shiver me timbers, we're home
and dry!

ONE: Noah took a clean pair of animals

SHEM: And put them on.

HAM: But they were far too tight.

JAPHETH: They were Noah constrictors.

TOGETHER: Sorry, sorry. We're very sorry.

TWO: And Noah let all the animals out of the ark.

ONE: Then he

TWO: And his family

ONE: Knelt down on top of the mountain

TWO: And thanked God for delivering them from judgement.

ONE: And God said:

GOD: Never again will I curse the ground because of
men, even though every inclination of his heart is evil
from childhood. And never again will I destroy all living
creatures as I have done. As long as the Earth endures,
seedtime and harvest, cold and heat, summer and winter,

day and night will never cease. I will set my rainbow in
the clouds.

SHEM: Hey, where's the rainbow?

JAPHETH: Somebody brought it on earlier.

NOAH: Ham?

HAM: Yeah?

NOAH: The rainbow.

HAM: What, the one on the table?

NOAH: Yes.

GOD: And whenever the rainbow appears in the clouds
. . . (*Firmly*) And whenever the RAINBOW appears in
the clouds . . . (*Exit* HAM, *sheepishly*) I will see it. I
will *see it*! (*Re-enter* HAM *with rainbow*) And remember
the everlasting covenant . . . (HAM *holds it up above
the group*)

ONE: Between God

TWO: And all living creatures

ONE: Of every kind

TWO: On the earth.

How to be a Hero

NARRATOR; GIDEON, *a young man somewhat lacking in physical presence*; ANGEL

This sketch is an interlude from The Grand Slam, *commissioned by the Pathfinder Organisation. Although written for children, it works equally well for an adult audience.*

Enter NARRATOR.

NARRATOR: Good evening. Here is the good news. No one is ever too small or too weak or too insignificant to work for the King of Kings. Take the story of Gideon for a start – Gideon was the youngest member of the smallest family in the least important tribe of Israel!! (*Enter* GIDEON, *nervously*)

GIDEON: Hello, I'm . . . er . . . well, (*Clearing his throat*) Gideon, actually. (*He laughs nervously*)

NARRATOR: But God chose Gideon to defeat the terrifying enemy, the Midianites!

GIDEON: (*Wheeling round*) Who me? (*The* ANGEL *enters*)

ANGEL: Yes, you.

GIDEON: (*Jumping back*) But . . . but . . . but . . . but have you seen the Midianites! Well, I suppose, being an angel you have seen the Midianites, ha, ha! But the point is, and this is where the crunch comes, those fellows are *big*, and when I say big, I mean – telephone directories in half, you know the stuff, and I . . . Well, quite honestly, I'm not even a seven stone weakling, I'm only a six and a half stone weakling and today is Tuesday.

ANGEL: Tuesday?

GIDEON: (*Sitting down*) Yes. Tuesday is my day off.

ANGEL: Gideon. Get up at once.

GIDEON: Yessir.

ANGEL: Now stop wasting time. When I say I want *you*

to blast the Midianites into smithereens, I mean *you*! Right?

GIDEON: Right!

ANGEL: You!

GIDEON: Me! . . . Right! Fine! . . . (*Beginning to go and then turning back*) Just one question.

ANGEL: What?

GIDEON: What about if I have measles?

ANGEL: Gideon, you do not have measles.

GIDEON: No. But I really wish I did have measles.

ANGEL: Gideon, even if you did have measles, you would still have to go and FIGHT THE MIDIANITES!

GIDEON: (*Going*) Right! Fight the . . . Midianites!! Right! (*Turning*) One more question.

ANGEL: (*Wearily*) What is it?

GIDEON: How do I know that all this isn't a joke, a sort of sick joke, you know, let's have a bit of a laugh, let's send that weedy, skinny little Gideon to fight the Midianites and watch him get hacked to pieces and all have a jolly good laugh. I mean, I wouldn't blame you. I'd be the first to make a total and utter fool out of somebody like me – now don't get me wrong – I just want a little bit of proof, that's all I'm asking, so . . . say I, er . . . lay out this sheepskin on the grass (*He takes off his sheepskin jacket*) and in the morning, there's dew on the sheepskin but not on the grass. That would be a miracle, right?

ANGEL: Right!

GIDEON: That would be proof, right?

ANGEL: Right!

GIDEON: Okay.

NARRATOR: So Gideon laid out the sheepskin and went to bed. (GIDEON *mimes winding up his alarm clock, cleaning his teeth and going to sleep*) And in the morning: Brrrrring! (GIDEON *wakes up, stops the alarm and checks the fleece*)

GIDEON: Curses! A miracle! Which means, you're right, I've got to fight the Midianites. Okay. Fair enough. But to fight the Midianites, people like me have got to be very sure that the Lord is on their side. So, what do you say,

we try it the other way round – dew on the grass and not
on the fleece? And it's a deal.

ANGEL: Done.

NARRATOR: So Gideon went back to bed. (GIDEON *mimes
winding up the alarm, cleaning his teeth, then says his
prayers – pointing to the sheepskin and shaking his head
– clearly praying that there won't be a miracle this time. He
goes to sleep*) And sure enough, in the morning: Brrrring!
(GIDEON *wakes up, stops the alarm, and checks the sheepskin. Then he checks the ground. He double-checks. Then he
crosses over his hands and tries checking the sheepskin and
the ground with a different hand*)

GIDEON: Curses! Another miracle!

NARRATOR: So after several more tests . . . (GIDEON *mimes
a sequence of childish tests: first he picks a flower, saying
'Yes', 'No', to himself as he removes the petals. He has
miscalculated. The verdict of the petals is 'Yes'. Then he
takes a coin and passes it rapidly from hand to hand
behind his back. Bringing both hands forward, he proceeds
to choose the hand without the coin. Deep frustration. Next
he tosses the coin into the air for 'heads or tails'. The
coin disappears into the sky, He looks accusingly at the*
ANGEL. *He gives up*) . . . Gideon had to go and fight the
Midianites!

GIDEON: Right. I'm getting a bodyguard. A bodyguard of
fifty thousand men. (GIDEON *stands at the side of the stage
and shouts orders to an imaginary vast army offstage. He
makes the sound of their tramping and improvises other
army effects*)

ANGEL: Er . . . Gideon?

GIDEON: Squaaaaaaad halt! (*He makes the sound of soldiers
standing to attention*) Yup?

ANGEL: Where are you going?

GIDEON: Just going to fight the Midianites.

ANGEL: Who are they?

GIDEON: Who?

ANGEL: Those soldiers.

GIDEON: (*Looking round, seeing his army as if by surprise
and jumping back*) Ohhh! Oh *those* soldiers . . . er . . . er

. . . some friends, you know . . . going to help, a few old
school chums, ha, ha!

ANGEL: Gideon, no school has that many pupils.

GIDEON: Comprehensive educa . . .? (*His voice trails off
into a nervous cough*)

ANGEL: Gideon, the Lord finds that huge army an insult to
his power. Get rid of it.

GIDEON: Er, right. (*He looks at his imaginary army offstage
and mimes dismissing three or four soldiers*)

ANGEL: Just keep a few.

GIDEON: What?

ANGEL: A *few*.

GIDEON: Er, right. (*He mimes recalling the three or four
soldiers and dismissing the huge army.* GIDEON *and the*
ANGEL *leave. As he goes* GIDEON *shouts:*) All right, lads!
Follow me. I'm behind you.

NARRATOR: Well, it's a very long story but the Lord proved
his point. Gideon, the youngest member of the smallest
family in the least important tribe of Israel, with a handful
of men, utterly defeated the Midianites. POW!! (GIDEON
leaps back onstage and throws his cap in the air)

GIDEON: It was nothing actually, well – when I say *nothing*,
I do of course mean, it was really quite something that God
should use *me*, you know, ha, ha!

NARRATOR: So that is the good news: the weaker you are,
the smaller you are, the more insignificant you feel, the
more the God of all creation wants to take your life and
make it dynamite!!

David and Goliath

NARRATOR; CHORUS (*anything from five to fifteen actors*)

This is a highly theatrical piece, requiring great energy and strong chorus interaction, which is difficult to convey fully in print. The sketch is built round the rhythm of an army on the march and was originally written for a children's service, though it works extremely well for audiences of all ages. The use of group narration, strong rhythm, sound effects and stylised action is an exciting combination and could be adapted for many other stories. It is a very reliable style, particularly for street theatre.

The sketch is performed by the CHORUS, of which the NARRATOR is the leader, and from which other, individual characters emerge as required. 'RHYTHM' indicates the sound of marching made by the CHORUS slapping their thighs and this keeps strictly to a repeated four-beat sequence – dadaDUM DUM DUM DUM, dadaDUM DUM DUM DUM etc; or musically (♫ ‖ . . . . ♫ ‖). 'FX' is shorthand for appropriate verbal sound effects. The giant GOLIATH can be made by draping a step-ladder with a cloth; an actor, wearing a helmet and huge rubber hands, stands on the ladder in such a way that only his head is visible above the cloth. An addition to this could be two other actors standing behind the cloth, each playing a leg and an arm, which they swing alternately in time to the rhythm. The sketch begins with the rhythm, started by the NARRATOR, picked up by the CHORUS, then fading away into the distance.

NARRATOR: In the days when men fought like animals.
CHORUS: (*FX Different animal noises*)
NARRATOR: And died like gnats.
CHORUS: (*FX VVZZZZZ Splat*)

NARRATOR: Men banded themselves together into great armies to teach each other a thing or two.

CHORUS: (*Rhythm*)

NARRATOR: Pillaging, ravaging, skirmishing, scavenging.

CHORUS: Pillaging, ravaging, skirmishing, scavenging.

NARRATOR: Now one day, (*rhythm stops*) King Saul of Israel was in his palace, eating his lunch.

CHORUS: (*With action*) Munch, munch, lovely lunch, munch, munch, lovely lunch, munch, munch.

NARRATOR: When news arrived.

CHORUS: (*FX Choking on lunch*) Whassat!??

NARRATOR: The Philistines are coming!

CHORUS: Oh, no! The Philistines are coming! (*Rhythm*)

NARRATOR: Now, in terms of fighting after lunch,
The Philistines were an ugly bunch.
They were the biggest in the land,
And Israelites they couldn't stand.
The Philistines got nearer and nearer and bigger and bigger. (*Rhythm louder*) The Israelites got smaller and smaller and paler and paler. (*Rhythm softer*) They shot their arrows.

CHORUS: (*FX Action firing two arrows*)

NARRATOR: But the arrows just bounced off the Philistines.

CHORUS: (*FX Arrows bouncing off armour*)

NARRATOR: So they threw their spears.

CHORUS: (*FX Action hurling spears*)

NARRATOR: But the spears just bounced off the Philistines.

CHORUS: (*FX Larger metal objects hitting armour. Rhythm*)

NARRATOR: And the Philistines stopped. 'Halt!'

CHORUS: Dadumpf!

NARRATOR: And the Israelites stopped. (*Quavering*) 'Halt!'

CHORUS: Dadumpf!

NARRATOR: And they glared at each other across the valley.

CHORUS: GLARE! GLARE!

NARRATOR: (*During this speech,* GOLIATH *sets himself*) Now, the Philistines had a sensational secret weapon. It was a man called Goliath, who was ten feet tall. Goliath was big for his age. You know the kind of guy who'd kick sand in your face at the seaside? Well, Goliath was the kind of guy who'd kick whole *beaches* in your face. And he had a horrible laugh.

CHORUS: (*Sonorously*) Huh, huh, huh, huh, HA, HA, AAAHH!

NARRATOR: Every day, they gave him a barnful of whole-wheat nourishment.

CHORUS: (*FX Action. One actor pitchforks two bales of food into* GOLIATH'S *mouth. Noisy eating*)

NARRATOR: Then he would march up and down the valley,

CHORUS: (*Rhythm.* GOLIATH *begins to march on the spot*)

NARRATOR: Shouting . . .

CHORUS: Come and fight me, come and fight me, scaredi-cats, scaredicats, nyeah, nyeah, nyeah. (*Repeat*)

NARRATOR: And in the silence, you could hear the Israelites' hearts beating.

CHORUS: (*FX Action*) BaBOM, baBOM, baBOM.

NARRATOR: No one would take up the challenge.

VOICE 1: Er, 'fraid not . . . bit too close to breakfast for me, old chap. Rice Krispies bobbing up and down, so er . . .

VOICE 2: Sorry. Gammy leg, I'm afraid.

VOICE 3: I've got a note from my mother. 'No games'.

NARRATOR: But Goliath continued to march up and down the valley.

CHORUS: (*Rhythm*)

NARRATOR: Shouting . . .

CHORUS: Come and fight me, come and fight me, scaredi . . .

DAVID: I'll fight you! (*He stands in front of group*)

VOICE 1: Who said that?

DAVID: I did.

VOICE 2: Where are you?

DAVID: Here.

NARRATOR: Where?

DAVID: HERE.

CHORUS: (*Derisive laughter*)

NARRATOR: It was David.

VOICE 3: Come off it. He's only someone's baby brother.

NARRATOR: But David was determined to go and fight Goliath.

CHORUS: (*Rhythm.* DAVID *picks this up with his feet*)

NARRATOR: He refused all the armour they offered him and trusted in God alone. He took his sling and five smooth stones. (DAVID *collects them*)

CHORUS: One, two, three, four, five. (*Rhythm*)

NARRATOR: When Goliath saw David coming towards him, he laughed his horrible laugh.

CHORUS: Huh, huh, huh, huh, HA, HA, AAAHH!

NARRATOR: And shouted –

GOLIATH: I'll pulverise yer, yer little squirt!

DAVID: I may be little, but God's on my side!

GOLIATH: SHUDDUUUPP!!

CHORUS: (*Rhythm*)

NARRATOR: So David took his sling, put a stone in it and FIRED.

CHORUS: (*FX Action, whirling sling four times*)

DAVID: Catch this one, Goliath.

CHORUS: (*FX Stone hitting forehead*)

NARRATOR: And Goliath caught it – right between the eyes – and crashed to the ground.

CHORUS: (*Cheering*)

NARRATOR: And when the Israelites saw that Goliath was dead and that God was on their side, they took heart.

VOICE 1: Oh, I say! Jolly good show!

VOICE 2: Wizard prang!

VOICE 3: Spiffing!

VOICE 4: Really wopped him there, David.

VOICE 5: Cracking fine shot!

NARRATOR: And the Israelites charged. 'Tally-ho!'

CHORUS: (*Sing opening bars of 'William Tell Overture'. Disintegrates into battle noise*)

NARRATOR: And the Philistines fled in panic.

CHORUS: (*FX Screams and pattering feet into distance*)

NARRATOR: So they shot their arrows after them.

CHORUS: (*FX Firing two arrows*)

NARRATOR: And they were all killed, to the last man.

VOICE 1: 'ERE, 'ang about. *I'm* the last man.

CHORUS: (*All fire arrows at him*)

VOICE 1: (*Sudden, St Sebastian-style death*)

CHORUS: (*Rhythm*)

NARRATOR: Why was Goliath so surprised when David hit him with a stone?

VOICE 2: Because nothing like that had entered his mind before.

NARRATOR: Please! What does the story teach us?

VOICE 3: To duck.

NARRATOR: (*Wearily*) Any sensible suggestions?

VOICE 4: To trust in God.

NARRATOR: Thank you!

CHORUS: (*Severally*) What a cracking good scheme. Just the ticket. Should have tried that one before. I'll say.

VOICE 3: Well, what about having a crack at it now?

NARRATOR: Why not?

CHORUS: (*With rhythm and words fading to silence*) Trust in God, trust in God, trust in God . . .

Snakes and Ladders

SON; FATHER; LOOSE WOMAN, *a party goer*; DOG-OWNER, *a patronising superior at work*; BALLOON-BLOWER, *a malicious friend.*

This text is printed without specific stage directions as an encouragement to experiment. It was first performed on Thames Television as a monologue. The actor was dressed as a harlequin and the set consisted of a gigantic snakes and ladders board, with a huge dice used as a seat. At the end of the sketch, the set 'vanished', leaving the harlequin sitting on his dice as if floating in space, thinking about flattery. Since its first performance it has been adapted for the stage and its most recent production device has been a photographic studio. The principal characters of the FATHER, *the* LOOSE WOMAN, *the* DOG-OWNER *and the* BALLOON-BLOWER *have been directed as a family group which the photographer (the* SON) *has been trying to pose. The introductory section of the sketch has been arranged as a series of snapshots; then each character, in turn, has emerged from the group to encounter the* SON *in their respective scenes. The group can (to choose one example) wreathe their hands like snakes round the* FATHER *as he describes the effect of flattery. However, there is nothing to stop a talented actor returning to the idea of a monologue – but he will need to evoke all the characters clearly.*

SON: There are some people in the world who never smile because they are depressed, angry, too clever, too busy to smile.

And there are some people who smile all the time because they are nervous or stupid or cunning or cruel. But most of us prefer to strike a balance.

We smile when something is funny when we see children playing in the park

when we are happy, when we are in love!
At other times we prefer to remain
serious
in hospital
in church
during the News at Ten.
If, however, we are to live a
peaceful life, we must learn to avoid the tricks of those who
smile too much
and among all those who smile too much we must learn to
distinguish the smile of the flatterer.
Now when I was a little child my father said to me:

FATHER: My son! Hear your father's instructions and pay
attention, that you may be wise. Be careful to do everything
I tell you and you will walk on your way securely and your
foot will not stumble. BEWARE OF FLATTERY! The
smiles of an enemy are worse than the criticisms of a
friend. The man who laughs at your jokes may stab you
in the back. The woman who praises your looks may seek
to destroy you. Do not be taken in! See how the flatterers
smile and nod and wink and pat you on the back and see how
they place their coils around you with every compliment,
like snakes!

SON: Now the first kind of flatterer I was warned about was
the simplest to detect. My father said to me:

FATHER: My son! Pay attention to my advice. The lips of
a loose woman drip honey and her speech is smoother
than oil but in the end she is as sharp as a two-edged
sword.

SON: Watch now, how she approaches! She is like a person
preparing to eat a delicious meal.

LOOSE WOMAN: How super to see you! Everybody's been
talking about you, all over the town. I've heard such a lot
about you!

SON: Her aim is to put me on a plate of my own self-esteem,
where she can liberally spread me with praise.

LOOSE WOMAN: I'm so excited to meet you.

SON: First, the plate.

LOOSE WOMAN: I've been longing to find out all about you.

SON: Then, the butter.

LOOSE WOMAN: You know, I thought you were very funny at that party last week but I didn't have the nerve to come and speak to you.

SON: Notice how thickly she spreads it on.

LOOSE WOMAN: I thought – he wouldn't want to come and speak to someone like *me*.

SON: After this, she pours on the honey.

LOOSE WOMAN: You're so witty, you know – so well-dressed – so clever at your work – so kind of you to stop and talk to me.

SON: Finally, she sandwiches me between her compliments and takes me home for supper.

LOOSE WOMAN: Your hair is incredibly soft.

SON: Munch.

LOOSE WOMAN: Your shoulders are so brown.

SON: Munch.

LOOSE WOMAN: So beautiful.

SON: Munch.

LOOSE WOMAN: So delicious.

SON: MUNCH MUNCH MUNCH. (*The* FATHER *intervenes*)

FATHER: It is not good to eat much honey so be sparing of complimentary words.

SON: Now the second kind of flatterer I was warned about was harder to detect. My father said to me:

FATHER: Watch out for the dog-owner, who ties you to a leash of flattery, who praises you to keep you under his control!

SON: See how the dog-owner approaches, like a man about to tame an animal.

DOG-OWNER: I would be extremely interested to know your opinion.

SON: As he listens attentively to what I am saying, he fixes on the collar.

DOG-OWNER: Is that so? How fascinating! Of course, you're a great expert at this sort of thing.

SON: Then, as he nods his head to every suggestion I make, he fixes on the leash.

DOG-OWNER: You're absolutely right.

SON: He says.

DOG-OWNER: I couldn't agree more.

SON: He says.

DOG-OWNER: I'm so glad I came to see *you*.

SON: He says. And now he takes me for a walk.

DOG-OWNER: I have tremendous confidence in your ability. You must feel free to come and chat to me at any time because obviously you've got a lot of important things to say.

SON: However, the dog-owner is not the slightest bit interested in what I have to say. He is merely enjoying taking me for a walk and tossing me a few scraps now and then to keep me quiet.

DOG-OWNER: I know I can depend on you.

SON: (*Gulp*)

DOG-OWNER: If more people were like you, my job would be easier.

SON: (*Gulp*)

DOG-OWNER: You're just the sort of person the world needs.

SON: (*Gulp*)

FATHER: The man who makes his neighbour look small is a fool.

SON: I have always kept to my father's advice and learnt how to recognise the art of the flatterer. Now the third kind of flatterer I was warned about was even harder to detect. My father said to me:

FATHER: Look out for the double-edged remark, the praise that pumps you up and up and up. Watch out for the balloon-blower!

SON: See how this man approaches, trapping me between his teeth like the neck of a balloon.

BALLOON-BLOWER: You're doing so well.

SON: He says.

BALLOON-BLOWER: How do you do it? How do you manage to keep so calm?

SON: He begins to blow: phhhhh!

BALLOON-BLOWER: To be so clever?

SON: Phhhhh!

BALLOON-BLOWER: To be so self-assured?

SON: Phhhhh!

BALLOON-BLOWER: To handle all the problems that you handle with such incredible ease?

SON: Phhhhh!

BALLOON-BLOWER: I wish I had half the ability that you have!

SON: He says. And now he pauses for breath.

BALLOON-BLOWER: Of course, I am the last person who should criticise *you* in any way.

SON: Phhhhh! I am nearly at my fullest extent, when – of course – he can destroy me with ease. He gives one final blow.

BALLOON-BLOWER: As you know, I've always agreed with everything you've ever done.

SON: Phhhhhhhhhhhh!

BALLOON-BLOWER: But some people are saying: such and such, and such and such, and such and such.

SON: BANG! I deflate to a pathetic rag. Having thus destroyed me with his criticisms, the balloon-blower commiserates.

BALLOON-BLOWER: I don't know what they're complaining about, myself.

SON: He discards the balloon.

BALLOON-BLOWER: Personally, I'd back you up all the way.

FATHER: There are friends who pretend to be friends, but under their lips is the poison of vipers.

SON: I am glad that my father warned me about flattery. He said:

FATHER: Be careful to do everything I tell you and then you will walk on your way securely and your foot will not stumble.

SON: I have kept to the ladders and avoided all the snakes, just as in the game. Of course, I have slipped up every now and then but we all do, don't we? We can't all be perfect. The main thing is to live one's life as best one can and if we do make a mistake we mustn't blame ourselves too much. No, by and large, I have lived a good, honest life – knowing when to be serious and when to smile.

When to be strict and when to be gentle.
When to work hard and when to relax
And how to avoid flattery.

FATHER: But the hardest flattery of all to detect is in yourself.

(*Blackout*)

THE BIBLE AND DRAMA

God's Word is active

The Bible is often referred to as 'the Word of God', but John's gospel speaks of Jesus Christ as the Word 'which became flesh and dwelt among us'. This is a statement for all time that God's Word is not a question of theory, a mere utterance, but is living and active, 'sharper than a two-edged sword'. The Bible is not so much a book of words but a book of actions, the actions of a Creator-God who is dramatic, who causes, who enters, who alters, who decides and who exemplifies his purposes clearly to human beings. God's ultimate action was the incarnation of the Messiah in human form.

The Bible therefore affirms that 'word' and 'action' are inextricably linked. Even the Hebrew word *dabar* means both 'word' and 'action'. The Bible is a poor manual for anyone interested in abstract philosophical speculation but it is a constant inspiration to all who wish to live out the life of the spirit and, furthermore, it is inspiration to those who seek to communicate God's Word with clarity today.

There are numerous instances in the Bible of words being used in a way which goes beyond that of mere information. In fact, there are only very few passages – perhaps some genealogies and tabulations of laws – where words are simply 'functional'. It is as if God's messages to man naturally find a form which is often an image, an illustration, a picture, a poem, a story told simply and dramatically. And it is no coincidence that Jesus, who was both the medium and the message of salvation, helped people to receive his words by telling them unforgettable parables and stories.

Christians have often emphasised *what* is said rather

than *how* it is said, with fatal consequences. Life is not
all 'head', it is body, mind, spirit and soul. We need
to convey the Christian message in such a way that
it will speak to the whole man. A careful study of the
Bible is the best possible education for anybody wishing
to do this.

The techniques of the prophets

The prophets knew how to use words memorably so that the
record of the divine will would stand the test of time, despite
its frequent initial rejection. Their prophecies were couched
in poetic form and contained every conceivable literary
device: puns, assonance, imagery, symbolism, quotations,
irony, sarcasm, and some of the greatest lyrical genius.
Not only did they speak the Word of God but they spoke it
with artistry – with God-inspired technique. They knew their
contemporary culture and they knew how to speak words
which would plunge like shafts of steel into the hardest
of hearts or would reach with loving sympathy into the
most desolate of predicaments. And as well as speaking
powerfully, they often added strength to their message by
performing symbolic actions: Ahijah's sign to Jeroboam of
the coat rent in pieces, Elijah's sign to Joash with the bow
and arrows, Isaiah's naming of his sons, Hosea's marriage to
Gomer, Jeremiah's breaking of the potter's vessel, Ezekiel's
brick-siege of Jerusalem. Nobody that God intended to hear
his Word could have failed to understand their message,
though many refused to obey it.

The Psalms in performance

Certain psalms suggest far more colour and ritual in their
original context than we would dare to give them in our
church services. We have often reduced them to the palest
echo of the shouts of rejoicing, the confident processions, or
the dramatic cries to God which may have been part of their

performance in ancient Israel. Psalm 24 is a good example of a liturgy containing elements of dramatic form and some of the oldest psalm literature, such as the Song of Deborah, is intriguing in this respect.

This subject is a question of historical debate, and opinions vary greatly as to the degree of 'dramatic' involvement there may have been in such ancient texts, but the Bible itself clearly indicates that some of these pieces were written to include music, dance and procession. Even if none of this was the case the very words of the psalms and other books like Job or the Song of Solomon demonstrate a powerful dramatic imagination: a literary form that sees conflicts, that asks questions and poses answers, that characterises 'the arrogant' or delights the heart of the lover with descriptions of her beloved.

The New Testament

In a book of sketches, so many of which are based on material from the gospels, it is superfluous to point out the dramatic nature of the gospel narratives. Yet this is sometimes overlooked by Christians who regard the theoretical style of some of the epistles as the only way to communicate. Doctrine, in the twentieth century, should be expounded with comparable intellectual rigour to the epistles of Paul – there is a greater need for this, in our wishy-washy intellectual climate, than ever before. But Jesus knew that the majority of people respond initially to images and to the loving warmth of the communicator rather than to point-to-point arguments. Contact is often made first of all through the imagination, and latterly through the intellect. Neither should be despised. A close reading of the epistles, in fact, shows there to be less of a divide from the gospels in literary form than appears at first sight. The whole book of James, the book of Jude, the book of Revelation, many passages in Paul's writings, including the 'poetic mountain top' of the New Testament in I Corinthians 13, and so on, employ powerful imagery – miniature parables – that communicate to the heart of man, to his general humanity, as well as to his intellect.

The Bible as a source book

With all this in mind, it is important to have a sensible attitude towards the Bible when using it as a source book for writing sketches. There is a right and a wrong kind of reverence for scripture. The wrong kind is so attached to the text, word for word as it stands, that dramatisation is impossible. In transposing print from a page into situations involving the actions of various characters, it is inevitable that some minor changes need to be made. The right kind of reverence will take the inspired Word of God and translate it into language and images that can be easily understood. If Jesus said in the first century that 'the Kingdom of Heaven is like *this*', then we need in the twentieth century to say that '*this*' is like 'this'; in other words, we create new parables that speak to our own generation. Scripture has not been tampered with or undermined but, on the contrary, it has been brought alive for its hearers. The heart of the message must remain the same, but it is nonetheless urgent to clarify potential obscurities and to provide a meaningful 'shell' for the 'kernel' of the truth. To associate such an approach with de-bunking trends in liberal theology can only be based on ignorance of the principles inherent in the Bible itself, where there are many examples of re-interpretation of themes, development of ideas and clarification of God's Word according to the needs of particular situations. The interpretation of the 'Day of the Lord' by different prophets is one example; Paul's commentary on Exodus 34:29–35 in 2 Corinthians 3:13 is another. Anyone involved in translating the Bible into a primitive language will understand the right kind of freedom that is required. A friend of ours, working with the Chorote Indians in the Chaco, Argentina, came up against the problem of the absence of abstract nouns in the language. 'Peace' had to be translated by the idea of 'hearing one another', which warring tribal chiefs do when they make peace. This is one example, but there are many others. The human imagination is one of the supreme resources given to us by our Creator. A redeemed imagination, inspired by the Holy Spirit, is the whetstone to keep our dramatisation of the Christian gospel sharp.

The Two Shepherds

THE ARCHANGEL GABRIEL; SHENKYN, *a young shepherd*; LEWIN, *a senior shepherd in his late forties*

This scene has often been performed by Riding Lights Theatre Company as a sketch in its own right. It is in fact an extract from a full-length Christmas play called The Tree That Woke Up, *which was first performed in 1975 by the Upstream Theatre Company at the Roses Theatre, Tewkesbury. It is a piece which will appeal to all ages – a modern expression of the old Mystery Play tradition where the sublime majesty of the incarnation is mingled with the simple comedy of everyday life. As the Mystery Plays demonstrate, the comedy is not a frivolous distraction from the heart of the story, but rather the reverse is true – we see the glory of God in Christ breaking into the folly and the comedy of human existence. When God came down to earth, he came first to the poor and the unsophisticated, to those who were nothing in the world's scale of value. It was a group of shepherds, awkward, humorous, badly-dressed, their faces red from living rough, smelling of sheep, who were the first to kneel and worship the Saviour of the world. They would never know why God had chosen them, nor would they be very good at explaining the experience to sceptical friends and neighbours, but they have been remembered down the years in one of the most beautiful paradoxes of the Christian faith.*

SHENKYN *and* LEWIN *should be dressed in the coarse clothes of any shepherd one might see on the hills of Cumbria or Wales.* LEWIN *has a bluff exterior which disguises a nevertheless affectionate relationship with his shepherd boy. Their first words are a reference to an ancient Cumbrian sheep count.*

(GABRIEL *enters in resplendent robes. He is an awesome presence, though his manner with the audience is kindly and faintly conspiratorial as he prepares them for the entrance of the shepherds*)

GABRIEL: Pay attention.
 My name is Gabriel,
 I stand in the presence of God
 Higher than all angels
 Except Michael.
 Are you ready?
 (*He gestures to the stage around him*)
 The fields outside Bethlehem. Two shepherds are look-ing for their sheep. (*We hear the sound of bleating and the distant cries of the shepherds*) Wait here. I'm going to tell them about the child that is to be born to Mary and Joseph.
 (*He steps aside and stands motionless.* SHENKYN *rushes on, out of breath*) (*He looks around wildly and begins to count sheep in the direction of the audience*)
SHENKYN: Wuntherum, twotherum, cockerum, cutherum (*pronounced 'queue-therum'*), shetherum, shatherum, wine-berry, wigtail . . . tarry diddle? Den? (*He sighs*) I've lost two sheep. (*He cheers up on seeing* GABRIEL)
 Excuse me, sir. Can you advise me? (*He is puzzled that* GABRIEL *makes no response; not even looking at him*)
 Parlez-vous anglais? (*Silence*) Sprechen Sie Deutsch? (*He starts to inspect this strange 'statue' more closely, unaware that* LEWIN *has entered behind him*)
LEWIN: Wuntherum, twotherum, cockerum, cutherum, shetherum, shatherum, wineberry, wigtail . . . tarry diddle? Den? Two of our best sheep. (*Calling the boy who is hidden behind* GABRIEL) Shenkyn! (SHENKYN *appears*) You nutcase! Leave you alone for half an hour and – chaos! Sheep jumping off the cliff, rushing into the woods, hiding in little holes.
SHENKYN: It always happens to me, sir.
LEWIN: Perhaps it's the look of your face, boy. Sheep are very choosy animals.
SHENKYN: Well, you can't blame me for that.
LEWIN: I can't blame the sheep, either. Wait, I'll ask

this gentleman if he's seen two sheep. (*Going over to* GABRIEL) Excuse me, sir, have you seen two sheep? (GABRIEL *remains unmoved, staring out into the audience*) Hello, hello?

SHENKYN: (*Helpfully*) I think he's foreign, Mr Lewin.

LEWIN: Yes, well, I've handled this sort of situation before. (*He steps back a few paces and addresses* GABRIEL *in the absurdly loud tones of the British tourist abroad*) HALLO! (*Changing to a French accent*) Allo! Bon. (*Moving closer and reverting to English*) Two. Yes? Sheep. SHEEP. Yes. Gone. Perdu. Kaput. No . . . idea? No. (*With sudden inspiration he attempts a sheep impression*) Hop, hop, baaaa. Good. Two hop, hop baaaas have, er, hopped it. (*He chuckles momentarily at his own joke, then gives up in disgust*) You have a go.

SHENKYN: (*Trying to catch* GABRIEL's *eye*) Excuse me, sir, we were wondering . . . Mr Lewin?

LEWIN: Yes?

SHENKYN: There's a strange glow on this man's face.

LEWIN: Don't worry about that. They've probably all got it where he comes from. Go on.

SHENKYN: Excuse me, sir, but we've lost two – wooo! (GABRIEL *moves for the first time, gesturing towards the sky.* SHENKYN *follows his arm*) M-M-Mr Lewin! (*He rushes back to* LEWIN) There's not just one of him now, there's a whole lot more!

LEWIN: I expect they're here on holiday. Now, go on.

SHENKYN: (*Turning nervously to look up at the sky*) Er, anyway, we . . . Mr Lewin.

LEWIN: Yes, what is it?

SHENKYN: (*Controlling a rising sense of panic*) There must be about five thousand of them by now and their eyes are red like fire and their hair as white as driven SNOW! MR LEWIN! (*He jumps into* LEWIN's *arms. They slowly disentangle themselves*)

LEWIN: (*With a calmness he does not feel*) Don't panic, boy. Try and speak to them.

SHENKYN: (*Hesitatingly he approaches the heavenly host*) Hello – everybody. Oh, Mr Lewin, there are thousands

upon thousands cascading from Heaven, laughing and
singing, with six wings, with eight wings, some small
as your little finger, others a hundred feet tall. Angels,
sir, angels!

LEWIN: It's not normal.

SHENKYN: No, sir, it's most unusual. I can see a door
in Heaven opened and from this door come thousands
upon thousands of people in great splendour. There are
horsemen and chariots circling the moon. Dogs baying and
every kind of animal and people coming like the waves of
the sea. Oh, Mr Lewin, I'm afraid that we've died and
gone to Heaven!

LEWIN: (*As they sink to their knees in prayer*) Oh, God, have
mercy upon us.

GABRIEL: (*Who has been watching all this*) Do not be afraid.
(*Both shepherds let out a yell of fear. They spin round
towards* GABRIEL, *collapsing in a heap. They are transfixed
as he speaks*) For, behold, I bring you good news of a great
joy which will come to all the people. For to you is born
this day in the city of David a Saviour, who is Christ the
Lord. And this will be a sign for you: you will find a babe
wrapped in swaddling clothes and lying in a manger. Glory
to God in the highest and on Earth peace among men with
whom he is pleased. (*He leaves.* LEWIN *and* SHENKYN *slowly
pick themselves up, as if awaking from a dream*)

LEWIN: I have seen a vision.

SHENKYN: Listen – the angels are singing 'Glory to God in
the highest'.

LEWIN: (*Gazing out into the night sky*) They are like the
clouds at sunset, layer upon layer, as each one falls back
the sky becomes more beautiful.

SHENKYN: The sound of their voices is like the thunder of
water showering into a mighty ocean.

LEWIN: The sound of their voices is like a waterfall of
golden coins.

SHENKYN: Rivers bursting into the desert.

LEWIN: Thunder upon thunder upon thunder.

BOTH: Glory to God in the highest and on Earth peace
among men with whom he is pleased.

SHENKYN: (*After a pause*) Look, dirt becoming a green leaf! (*He touches the ground beside him*) A piece of dust turning into a flower.

LEWIN: This singing will change the universe into Paradise.

SHENKYN: (*Getting up*) Oh, God, that you have granted this to us! Me and Mr Lewin!

LEWIN: And to think, Lord, that you have come to dwell on Earth in a humble stable, when you could have had a bedroom in my house, with Annie, Jim, Dick and Peter . . .

SHENKYN: (*Interrupting him gently*) The singing has stopped now. I'll never hear anything like that again.

LEWIN: My wife isn't going to believe this. Not likely. (*Mimicking her*) 'Angels! Oh, yes, and do you know what time it is?' Bop, bop. (*He cowers from an imaginary rolling-pin*) Angels!

SHENKYN: How do you explain them, Mr Lewin?

LEWIN: You don't explain them, Shenkyn, you can't – I mean: 'Sorry I'm late, my dear, but we've just seen about three million angels singing hallelujah, peace on Earth and goodwill to everybody down here.'

SHENKYN: You can't really, can you?

LEWIN: We'll have to break it to them gently, piece by piece, it's a very shocking thing, truth.

SHENKYN: Oh.

LEWIN: Yes. What with the present state of affairs, it's a rare commodity and very upsetting when it happens. Upsets the routine. Puts it right out of action.

SHENKYN: It can mean that you miss supper altogether. Well, what are we going to say?

LEWIN: We'll say . . . 'There was this stable – ' No, we'll . . . we'll get to the door and say, 'My goodness me, just look at the time!' No. No, we'll say, 'A funny thing happened to me on the way – ' No.

SHENKYN: But you know what the missus will say, anyway.

LEWIN: I do. But I won't let her. I'll say my bit. It's not every day that God gives you an excuse to be late like this. I'll say to her quite simply and she'll understand, 'All these angels came along to tell me . . . that God has come into the world and, um, I've been along to see him in this, er, small stable . . .'

SHENKYN: And you know what she'll say?

LEWIN: I've a feeling I do.

SHENKYN: She'll say . . .

LEWIN: God in a stable?

SHENKYN: Flippin' fable!

BOTH: And get your feet down off the table!

LEWIN: Come on. (*They go off to Bethlehem singing the first few lines of* 'Good Christian Men Rejoice')

Stable Talk

MARY; JOSEPH; (*also, if the final scene is used*) LEWIN, *a senior shepherd*; SHENKYN, *a shepherd boy*

This sketch originally appeared in Red Letter Days *as a monologue for Joseph, talking to the baby Jesus not long after his birth. Here it has been developed into a scene which can be performed as an immediate sequel to the previous sketch* The Two Shepherds. *It includes a brief re-appearance of the two shepherds themselves as they arrive at the stable in response to Gabriel's message. This is, of course, optional and the sketch can end perfectly well at the place indicated in the text.*

It is hard to dissociate the biblical account of the birth of Jesus from the welter of cosy Christmas card images which spring into our minds. The stable is no longer the worst accommodation available to the young couple, cold and smelling of cow dung; it has become invitingly warm, full of fresh hay and suffused with glorious lanternlight. It is therefore worth considering how to create an image of MARY *and* JOSEPH *which will resonate in the minds of your audience with a twentieth-century idea of youth, vulnerability and homelessness.*

As the sketch begins, MARY *is rocking the baby Jesus in her arms. Her quiet mood of delight and wonder in her child contrasts with* JOSEPH'S *frustration at their situation in Bethlehem – all that he would not have wished for the birth of* MARY'S *baby. It is the unfamiliar but tender experience of holding this baby, with whom he has had such an unusual fatherly relationship, that transforms his feelings.*

MARY: (*Talking to the baby*) If you could open your eyes, I'd show you a lovely star, wouldn't I?
JOSEPH: Through the holes in the roof.
MARY: (*Ignoring* JOSEPH) What a fine time to come, eh?

I had a feeling you were going to do this to us. I wanted a nice room all ready for you, see? Your father could make you a bed, couldn't he?

JOSEPH: Who?

MARY: You could.

JOSEPH: What kind of a bed?

MARY: Proper little bed. On rockers. With a little lamb carved into the headboard. (*To the baby*) Don't think your father wanted you to be stuck in this old vegetable box.

JOSEPH: (*Has come closer and is staring at the baby*) I wish I was your father.

MARY: Do you want a go with him?

JOSEPH: (*Taking baby gently but awkwardly*) I'm just standing in, like, for someone else. You know what I think? (*He takes the baby off for a private chat*), I think you are going to have your real father's temperament, because, you see, your father is a loving, kind, mighty, glorious, everlasting God. (*Pause*) And – the angel in my dream told me that you are going to save your people from their sins . . . seems a lot to ask of a little feller like you. But I think I shall be pretty proud of you anyway. You're still part of my family, you see. And it's a good family. Oh, ay. We go back a long way. I may only be a carpenter, but my great, great, great, great, great grandfather was king. There. He was. King David. (*Musing to himself*) We've had kings, priests, farmers, carpenters . . .

MARY: . . . And now we've got a king again.

(*The sketch could end at this moment. Alternatively*: SHENKYN *and* LEWIN *have entered behind them.* LEWIN *coughs*)

LEWIN: We didn't want to disturb you.

SHENKYN: But we wanted to see the little 'un!

LEWIN: Sssh! Wait till you're asked!

JOSEPH: He belongs to you as much as to me. Come in.

LEWIN: Aaah! Look, he's smiling.

SHENKYN: No, he's not.

LEWIN: He is, then. Look.

SHENKYN: Impossible, Mr Lewin. Newborn babies don't

know how to smile, you know. They don't learn that till about three weeks. That's wind.

LEWIN: You're not talking about any old baby, you know.

SHENKYN: So?

LEWIN: This baby is the Son of God. He's bound to be a bit different.

MARY: You can hold the baby if you like.

SHENKYN: We heard such music in Heaven for this child. Cloud upon cloud of angels singing, 'Glory to God in the highest'.

LEWIN: I have never seen such a face as this. All the kingdoms of the world would not do for this little child. Lord, have mercy upon us and grant us your peace.

SHENKYN: Remember us when you come into your kingdom . . . David Shenkyn.

LEWIN: Thomas William Lewin.

SONG: Sing, sing all earth
Sing, sing all earth eternal.
Praises sing to our Redeemer,
To our Redeemer and our heavenly king.

For us a Saviour came on earth.
For us his life he gave,
To save us from eternal death,
To raise us from the grave.

(This lyric is an extract from a traditional Christmas song sung by all the cast. Other songs or carols could also be appropriate)

The God Slot

CHAIRMAN; HILARY SCOTT, *a television producer*; JIM, *a novice broadcaster*

This sketch was originally broadcast in the comedy film WARP, *made for Central Television and featuring members of the Riding Lights Theatre Company.* WARP *(Worldwide Anglican Renewal Project) was an imaginary centre, where bishops could send their clergymen on training courses to 'face up to the twentieth century'. Therapy was on offer for anyone showing tendencies towards orthodox Christianity. A variety of refresher courses was on the curriculum, including one on the techniques of religious broadcasting.* JIM *was portrayed as a benign clergyman (he could be a lay person) experiencing his first training session under* HILARY SCOTT, *an extrovert and domineering TV producer. Although the original was set in a television studio with cameras and lights, for theatrical purposes it can be treated as a mock-up, the only prop necessary being a chair. The best way of involving the audience is to treat them all as conference members, and to pre-arrange a few people to carry scripts, which* HILARY *can collect during her demonstration.*

Enter CHAIRMAN *followed by* HILARY SCOTT. *He steps forward to address the audience.*

CHAIRMAN: May I welcome you all to 'Medium with a Message', our conference on the crisis facing religious broadcasting? Over the next few days, various experts will be giving a course of lectures ranging from how to keep religion on the air, how to preserve the image of Christianity as a sentimental singsong on Sundays, and finally how to earn a living as an ex-nun by working out personal grievances towards God on Channel Four. Our first guest is Hilary Scott, who has worked on pretty well every religious programme: *Stars on Sunday*, *Songs of Praise*, *Encounter*, *Heart of the Matter*, *Everyman*, *The Rock Gospel Show*, *Credo*, *Highway*, *The Money Programme* – in fact, there's very little that she doesn't know about worship in television. (*Turning to* HILARY) Hilary, welcome.

HILARY: Thank you, Donald. It's lovely to be here.

CHAIRMAN: Now I know you only have a few minutes before rushing back to the studio in London, for tonight's edition of *Doubt and Dogma*, so what advice would you offer to beginners in religious broadcasting?

HILARY: Well, Donald, I prefer not to offer advice. I like to demonstrate. Television is about pictures. About seeing for *ourselves*, and so I'd like to demonstrate a few techniques.

CHAIRMAN: That sounds marvellous.

HILARY: Some of us have been working very hard this afternoon, in a workshop on religious epilogues, and what I'm going to do now is collect a few of the scripts and then commandeer a volunteer.

CHAIRMAN: (*Taking his position in the audience*) Over to you, then.

HILARY: (*Breezily*) Right, have we all done our little bit? (*Various members of the audience hold up their scripts, which she collects*) 'Facing up to Bereavement', Keith. Good. 'Coping with an Elderly Relative', Susan. That's marvellous. 'The Crisis of Confidence in Western Democracy and the Critical Function of Neo-Marxist Praxis in the Context of Liberation Theology in Ecuador.' Not really suitable for pensioners in Whitstable, is it, Colin? I did say 'the average viewer', not the top six members of Mensa. Right? Jim, 'The Message of Christmas'. Super. And Barbara, 'Why Will No One Listen to Me?'

(HILARY *leafs through forty closely-handwritten pages*) Yes . . . Okay, would anyone except Barbara like to volunteer? (JIM *puts his hand up*) Jim. 'The Message of Christmas.' Wonderful. (*She beckons* JIM *up to the front and sits him on the chair*) Well done, Jim, it takes a lot of courage, even in a training session. Now, I've said it lots and lots of times, but I shall say it again, and I shall keep saying it, 'Try to forget the cameras.' (*Turning to the audience*) Okay, everyone? Jim, you look marvellous. Lean back, relax, darling. You're at home. Speaking to someone else in their home. And *cue*!

JIM: Hello. Christmas is full of wonderful things. Carols by candlelight, turkeys, presents, stockings –

HILARY: Hold it. You can cut all that out, Jim. It's waffle. It's padding. Get to the point. We've only got five minutes.

JIM: Yes, right, er . . . Hello. Have you ever wondered what it would be like to meet an angel?

HILARY: Relevance, darling. Keep it relevant and simple and inside the experience of the viewer.

JIM: Right, er . . . There was this . . . person, who went up to the Virgin Mary and –

HILARY: I don't think we want to stir up a hornets' nest of problems in our little five minutes' broadcast, do we? Remember, our aim is to simplify, to reach the lowest common denominator, and then go below it. All right? And *cue*!

JIM: And the person said to the young girl, he shall be called Jesus and shall be a light to all people.

HILARY: Jim, darling. I really have got to stop you again. Now, *think* about it.

JIM: What?

HILARY: 'A light to *all* people?' Was that very sensitive to our minority groups? Try to think of something that would be of equal appeal to a single white mother of two, a Rastafarian, a Jewish rabbi, a middle-aged couple in Hornsea and a 78-year-old Iranian member of the Baha'i faith. All right? Good. (*Turning to the audience*) A round of applause for a marvellous guinea-pig. (JIM *looks round, puzzled, then – realising this refers to him – shuffles back to his seat in the audience. The* CHAIRMAN *joins* HILARY)

CHAIRMAN: Well, it's easy to see why Hilary has had such a successful career in religious television. (*Turning to her*) Have you any final comment for us tonight?

HILARY: Yes. The important thing is to communicate. People come to me burning with a message, but no way of communicating it. Television reverses that process. It gives them a burning desire to communicate, but absolutely nothing to say. This is easily the best way to avoid offence and keep religious programmes on the air.

CHAIRMAN: Hilary Scott, thank you very much. (*He leads the audience in applause, then escorts her offstage*)

Wise Men from the West

READER OF THE LESSON; DOREEN PAPP *and* KEVIN MOZA-
RELLA, *astrologers*

*This sketch begins with a reading from an imaginary book of
the Bible, commenting on the folly of some of our practices
in the West. If performed during a service of worship, it is
essential that it is quite clearly announced as a sketch before
the 'reading' takes place, to avoid any unnecessary shock to the
congregation, who (if not prepared) might take offence at the
parody. Needless to say, this little monologue that prefaces the
main sketch can be treated as a one-minute cameo performance
on its own. The main sketch that follows should be staged like
a radio or TV breakfast show, with the resident astrologers
making their predictions to microphones, or unseen cameras,
and a studio audience. They are self-consciously 'show-biz',
with extravagant clothes –* DOREEN, *heavily made-up, with
huge glasses and dangly earrings,* KEVIN *with a loud suit
and rather dinky little shoes, somewhat camp and OTT.
However, actors should beware of over-acting parts like these.
Extroversion of this kind needs some subtlety of interpretation,
otherwise it can become irritating to the audience and the
performance may stand in the way of the material.*

KEVIN *and* DOREEN *should not take their seats until the reading
is over. The* READER *should be in Sunday best, treating his or
her task with dignity. Good timing is needed, but the manner
should follow traditional church readings as closely as possible,
straight-faced, avoiding any awareness of the comedy.*

The READER *approaches the lectern, turns over the pages of
the 'Bible' solemnly, and reads.*

READER: Now it came to pass in those days that certain
wise men arose in the West, saying, 'Behold, we have

seen the stars, even as it has been foretold, and verily, Tuesday
will be a lucky day for Sagittarians.' And the people marvelled
greatly, and were exceedingly impressed, and in like manner
they too consulted the stars and did come up with a load of
rubbish, yea verily, a pack of lies, so that the primitive tribes
of the Earth murmured among themselves, saying, 'If this
is where Western civilisation has got the human race, you
can keep it, mate.' Notwithstanding, a great multitude of the
Western press, and other mighty organs of the media, did
daily publish abroad the sayings of the astrologers, so much
so that the wise men from the East were all but forgotten,
and the Star of Bethlehem became only a dim memory, and
the crying of a child in a manger was drowned by the clink
of money, crossing the palms of the false prophets. And in
those days a deep darkness fell upon the face of the land.

The READER *closes the 'Bible' and returns to his seat.
Ideally, a jingle (live or recorded) should introduce* DOREEN
and KEVIN, *with a voice-over: 'Ladies and gentlemen, will
you please welcome Kevin Mozarella and Doreen Papp.'
Canned applause.*

KEVIN: Thank you and welcome to another edition of *Star
Turns*, Britain's number one programme for predictions.
Well, Doreen, what do you think of the remarkable zones
of astral energy in the Milky Way this morning?

DOREEN: Astonishing, Kevin. A magical mix of the sun,
the new moon and Mercury, with Mars parallel to Pluto,
Venus conjoined to Saturn, and the electric vibes of Jupiter
throbbing across the asteroid belt.

KEVIN: Any thoughts about a general forecast for the
future?

DOREEN: Well, first of all, I think we can safely assume
that all star signs will experience a number of features in
common.

KEVIN: Such as?

DOREEN: Most people will either receive an unexpected
caller, make an important decision and have an upsurge of
romantic feelings, or experience none of these things at all.

KEVIN: Can we take this as a likely prediction?

DOREEN: Oh, I think so, Kevin. Most people will also spend a few minutes every day in a small room, apart from others, and this will be a significant time, depending on the reading matter available. In addition to this, over three million people will not face important business decisions in the coming year, and the fourteenth, seventeenth and twentieth days of the month will be lucky days for those who are employed, as will every other day.

KEVIN: Now it's time for our 'Alternative Sources of Information' spot, and it's back to you, Doreen, to tell us a little bit about the ancient art of divining the future from the entrails of animals.

DOREEN: Thank you, Kevin. Well, I've been taking a quick look at some chicken livers, sheep's intestines and rabbit droppings (*She produces a nasty-looking bag, probably not transparent*) and I think it would be fair to say that these have a lot more to say about the future than the average religious programme on television.

KEVIN: (*Peering into the bag*) I'm intrigued by those chicken livers, Doreen.

DOREEN: So was I. In fact, they made a nasty mess on the kitchen floor this morning when I threw them over my shoulder, and this usually means that there are problems ahead, especially for the chickens.

KEVIN: Finally, a letter from Mr K. Herod of Jerusalem. (*Reading*) 'Dear Kevin, I am worried about my future. Some men with silly hats on and funny accents came round the other day, and asked to see the King of the Jews. I thought it was a practical joke and I laughed heartily. However, it soon became clear that they did not know I was the King of the Jews and, worse than that, they insisted they were looking for a little baby. At this, I stamped my feet and screamed for my mother, but this did not convince them, and they went off to Bethlehem. Since then, things have been very quiet in Jerusalem, and the worship has fallen off considerably. What should I do? Yours sincerely, K. Herod.' Well, Mr Herod, if I am right in thinking that you are a Libran, the best thing is to believe in yourself. Have confidence. If you are the King of the Jews, don't shout about it, just be what you are. As for these rumours, I think the best thing is to stifle them wherever possible. (*Turning to Doreen*) What do you think?

DOREEN: I agree with Kevin, here. There is always someone who comes along and tells you that you've got it all wrong. Have confidence in yourself, your own philosophy, your own destiny. Don't bother with ridiculous superstitions.

KEVIN: So squash those doubts and fears thoroughly, Mr Herod. Kill off every suspicion that you may be wrong. That's all we have time for, today – oh! (*Turning over the letter*) There's a PS here. 'Do you know anything about the star over Bethlehem?' (*Shrugging his shoulders and looking at Doreen, who shakes her head*) We haven't heard of that at all, and it certainly doesn't appear in our charts, but I shouldn't worry. It's probably a bit of grit on your telescope. That's all from *Star Turns*, so from Doreen and myself, good morning.

DOREEN: Goodbye.

(*Repeat jingle, with canned applause, as they leave*)

The Parable of the Talents

NARRATOR ONE; NARRATOR TWO; DRACULA; FRED, *a hard-working gardener*; TED, *an astute salesman*; JULIAN POTTER-TON–BROWN, *a self-preoccupied fop*; THE MASTER, *a stern but kindly landlord*

As with other sketches which employ the 'two NARRATORS *plus mime' technique (see 'What to do on a Rainy Day' or 'In the Nick of Time'), the action has largely been left for you to devise. The style is well tried and tested and is useful for groups with actors who cannot learn lines, have to perform in buildings with poor acoustics, or who enjoy street theatre.*

ONE: Matthew

TWO: Twenty-five

ONE: Verse

TWO: Fourteen.

ONE: The parable of THE TALONS! (*Dramatic music. Enter* DRACULA *in evening dress, with swirling cape and long talons on his fingers. He threatens the audience melodramatically. The two* NARRATORS *confer*)

TWO: (*Explaining to the audience*). I'm sorry, apparently what we've got here is the parable of the *talents*.
(*Exit* DRACULA, *mortified that his moment of glory has been cut short. One of the* NARRATORS *can improvise, using the ordinary name of the actor: 'It was a nice idea, Geoffrey, but . . .'*)

ONE: Begin again.

TWO: Matthew

ONE: Twenty-five

TWO: Verse

ONE: Fourteen.

TWO: Jesus told a story

ONE: About

TWO: A man

ONE: Who had

TWO: Three servants – for the sake of argument:

ONE: Fred,

    (*Pause while* FRED *enters and takes up position*)

TWO: Ted,

    (*Pause while* TED *enters and takes up position*)

ONE: And Julian Potterton–Brown.

    (*Longer pause while* JULIAN POTTERTON–BROWN *makes a fastidious entrance*)

TWO: Now Ted was smarter than Fred.

ONE: But Fred was bigger than Ted.

TWO: Ted had a head to earn him his bread

ONE: Which cannot be said for Fred.

TWO: But Fred often said:

ONE: 'I don't 'ave Ted's 'ead.

TWO: I manage wiv muscles instead.'

ONE: Now Julian Potterton–Brown

TWO: Was the odd one out.

ONE: But this didn't deter him – after all:

TWO: 'I'm frightfully well-bred,' he said.

ONE: 'I'm greasier than Ted,' he said.

TWO: 'I'm lazier than Fred,' he said.

ONE: 'And I don't rhyme with either of them, the creeps.'

TWO: One day their employer summoned them to his office.

    (*Enter* THE MASTER. *He sits at a desk*)

ONE: Knock, knock.

TWO: 'Come in.

ONE: Now listen you three.

TWO: Fred, Ted and Julian whateveryourname is.'

ONE: (JULIAN *prompting him*) 'Potterton–Brown.'

TWO: 'Granted.'

ONE: 'Before I go away on my journey

TWO: I wish to give you each some money to look after.

ONE: Form a queue, form a queue.

    (JULIAN *makes sure he gets to the front, but* THE MASTER *bypasses him and goes straight to* FRED *at the end of the queue*)

TWO: Five talents for you.

ONE: Two talents for you. (*Given to* TED)

TWO: And one talent for you.' (JULIAN *looks at it disparagingly*)

ONE: So he waved goodbye.

TWO: He took his toothbrush.

ONE: Took his hat.

TWO: Took his coat.

ONE: Took his leave

TWO: And left.

    (*Exit* MASTER)

ONE: Now Fred had two thousand five hundred pounds.

TWO: Ted had one thousand pounds.

ONE: Julian had five hundred pounds.

TWO: But what were they going to do with it?

ONE: Fred had a flair for gardening and fancied growing some vegetables.

TWO: Ted had a flair for marketing and fancied his chances in business.

ONE: Julian had flares and fancied himself.

TWO: Fred rolled up his sleeves

ONE: Grabbed his money

TWO: And blew the whole lot on a spade

ONE: A garden shed

TWO: A plot o' land

ONE: A bag o' bulbs

TWO: An 'osepipe

ONE: And a pair of wellies.

TWO: And got stuck in.

ONE: The wellies.

TWO: Wellies not often that you . . .

ONE: Oh shut up.

TWO: Sorry. Ted surveyed the market very carefully.

ONE: Bided his time

TWO: Picked his moment

ONE: Got his wallet

TWO: Laid all his money on twenty

ONE: Second-'and camels.

TWO: Julian was sensible

ONE: Was wise
TWO: Was cautious
ONE: He considered the problems
TWO: The pitfalls
ONE: The dangers that lay ahead
TWO: The risk of losing everything.
ONE: And so Julian used his intelligence
TWO: He thought
ONE: He planned
TWO: He schemed
ONE: He did
TWO: Nothing.
ONE: Nothing.
TWO: But he was jolly careful with his money.
ONE: He wrapped it up in a silk handkerchief
TWO: On a velvet cushion
ONE: In a little box
TWO: And hid it under the floorboards.
ONE: And then:
TWO: A few years later:
ONE: Knock, knock.
TWO: Who's there?
ONE: Who do you think?
TWO: The master!
ONE: (*Gasping*) The master!
TWO: Quick, quick, form a queue, form a queue.
ONE: Same to you.
TWO: Shut up.
ONE: Shut up yourself.
TWO: Sssssh!
ONE: Ssh!

(*During this kerfuffle* JULIAN *has made sure, in contrast to the previous line-up, that he is at the back*. THE MASTER *returns*)

TWO: And the master called each man to account for the money he had entrusted to him.
ONE: 'Who's first?'

(FRED, *finding himself at the front of the queue, reluctantly comes forward*)

TWO: 'Well, it's not as much as I'd hoped, master, cabbages
       got frostbitten last year . . .'

ONE: 'Never mind that – well done, good and faithful
       servant!

TWO: You have doubled the money I gave you.

ONE: Enter into the joy of your Lord.

TWO: Next.'

       (TED *comes forward*)

ONE: 'Yeah – well – er, second-'and camels – sold a few,
       bought a few, crashed a few – but you can't win 'em all,
       so 'ere you are.'

TWO: 'Well done, good and faithful servant!

ONE: You too have doubled the money I gave you.

TWO: Enter into the joy of your Lord.

ONE: Next.'

       (JULIAN *takes out a prepared speech*)

TWO: (*Loud cough*)

ONE: (*Sound of clearing throat*)

       (JULIAN *applies a throat spray*)

TWO: 'Master!

ONE: My Lord!

TWO: (*Ingratiatingly*) Master . . .

ONE: Knowing you to be a hard man, etc., etc.

TWO: Blah blah blah, reaping where you did not sow

ONE: Blah blah blah, gathering where you did not winnow

TWO: Ploughing where you did not . . .
       (*Fighting for words*) plough, and so on . . .

ONE: And so forth . . .

TWO: I was afraid and hid the money.

ONE: I remain your obedient servant, Julian Pott – '
       (*His speech is cut short by* THE MASTER *snatching the paper
       from his hand and tearing it up. If the paper is mimed, one
       of the narrators should make a suitable ripping noise*)

TWO: 'You did nothing!

ONE: You're all words.

TWO: You're all talk.

ONE: All that I gave you has not grown one inch!

TWO: Take away the talent and give it to the man who
       has ten.

ONE:　And take this wicked servant and cast him into outer
　　　darkness.
　　　(JULIAN *is dragged offstage by invisible forces.* THE MASTER
　　　turns, as if to address the audience)
TWO:　Don't be deceived.
ONE:　Put everything that God has given you to good use.
TWO:　For one day you will have to give an account of
　　　your life
ONE:　To him.'

The Parable of the Good Punk Rocker

NARRATOR; CHORUS, *anything from five to fifteen actors*

This is a difficult sketch to transcribe, probably because it is the very opposite of a 'literary' style. It is a theatrical piece which depends on very strong chorus interaction, arranged round the rhythm of a railway train. Rhythm is present in all theatre in some form or another, usually through speech rhythms, but here it is deliberately exaggerated as a means of communicating memorably – just as the strong rhythms of nursery rhymes with chorus actions are so easy to remember. The piece is an attempt to put the story of the Good Samaritan into the context of an alienated member of modern society, but naturally – as fashions change – the sketch could be adapted. At the time of this re-publication, Punk is undergoing something of a revival, but other rebellious musical styles may seem more appropriate to the era of your performance!

The piece is performed by the CHORUS *from which the principal parts emerge when required. The* NARRATOR *should be one of the* CHORUS *and act as its leader. 'Rhythm' indicates the sound of a railway train made by the* CHORUS *with their hands slapping their thighs, 'FX' is shorthand for appropriate sound effects and actions. Each group will need to work out for itself the precise cues for the rhythm starting and finishing.*

NARRATOR: There was a man on a train from London to York. (*Rhythm*)
CHORUS: London to York – London to York – London to York – London to York.
NARRATOR: And as he sat down to read the newspaper he fell among football fans.
CHORUS: (*FX Football chant, clapping rather than singing. Repeat*)
NARRATOR: Who had just seen their team lose the cup.

CHORUS: BOO!! What a load of rubbish! (*Sung rather than said*)

NARRATOR: So they mugged the man and took his wallet and his coat. (*Four of the* CHORUS *mug the man with stylised blows accompanied by*)

CHORUS: OOH-OOH, AAH-AAH, OOH-OOH, AAH-AAH. (*FX Football chant*) You'll never walk again, a-gain. (*Rhythm*)

NARRATOR: Now on that train there was a vicar.

CHORUS: (*Singing*) A – a – men.

NARRATOR: Who felt sorry for the man.

CHORUS: (*FX Four sniffs*)

NARRATOR: So he hid in the lavatory and said a prayer.

CHORUS: SLAM! CLICK! (*The sounds are produced, rather than the words being said but there should be accompanying actions. Rhythm*)

NARRATOR: And also on that train there was a social worker from Camden Town who had wide experience with delinquents.

VOICE: I really care about the kids. (*She takes a drag on her fag*)

CHORUS: I really care about the kids. (*They all take a drag*)

NARRATOR: She cared so much about the kids that she went to the bar and had a drink.

CHORUS: (*FX Gulp. Rhythm*)

NARRATOR: Also on the train there was the leader of a punk rock band called 'The Dregs'.

CHORUS: (*FX Punk rock*)

NARRATOR: He was the meanest of the mean no-good guys.

CHORUS: (*FX Throwing up or something else suitably off-putting*)

NARRATOR: But he stopped the train.

CHORUS: (*FX Screech. Hiss*)

NARRATOR: Phoned the ambulance.

CHORUS: (*FX Phoning, followed by approaching siren*)

NARRATOR: Gave him thirty quid for a new coat.

CHORUS: (*Sympathetically*) Ahhh!

NARRATOR: And sent him off to hospital.

CHORUS: (*FX Siren fading off. Rhythm*)

NARRATOR: Now where that man came from there were no punk rockers.

CHORUS: (*FX Scandalised uppercrust*) Eaohh!

NARRATOR: But there was a vicar.

CHORUS: (*Singing*) A – a – men.

NARRATOR: And several social workers.

CHORUS: I really care about the kids. (*They all take a drag*)

NARRATOR: But when it came to the crunch.

CHORUS: (*FX Loud crunch*)

NARRATOR: Who was that man's real next-door neighbour? Yes?

VOICE: The one that *did* something for him!

CHORUS: Oh yes! The one that *did* something for him!

NARRATOR: Who showed (*with easy 'click' beat*) love, love, love, love. Love, love, love, love.

CHORUS: Love, love, love, love. Love, love, love, love.

NARRATOR: Jesus said: Go!!

CHORUS: (*Four clicks*)

NARRATOR: And do the same.

CHORUS: Love, love, love your neighbour! Love, love, love your neighbour! (*Rhythm*)

VOICE: Sir . . . sir . . . please, sir?

NARRATOR: (*Patiently*) What is it, Nigel?

VOICE: Who is my neighbour?

NARRATOR: Two, three:

CHORUS: EVERYBODY!!

VOICE: Oh yeah (*he laughs idiotically*) . . . (*Rhythm. Gradually fading as the actors sing a few lines of the gospel song* 'This train is bound for glory . . .')

A Little Advice from the Mount

This is a short reading from Not-the-Sermon-on-the-Mount. It aims to satirise the prevailing mood of Britain in the late twentieth century by deliberately twisting the revolutionary teaching of Jesus so severely that the truth of the original can be felt even more keenly by contrast. It can be delivered as an alternative 'reading from scripture', though care must be taken, if this is performed in the context of a church service, to ensure the audience are prepared for the harsh nature of the satire. Occasionally, the use of a national accent can give this piece an additional edge where the nation in question could legitimately be said to pay lip-service to the Christian religion, while behaving heartlessly towards its neighbours or citizens.

Seeing the state of the nations, he went up on the mountain and when he sat down the world leaders came to him. And he opened his mouth and taught them through the mass media, saying, 'You have heard that it was said, "An eye for an eye and a tooth for a tooth." But I say unto you, Why stop there? Resist one who is evil. If anyone strikes you on the right cheek, have you not cause enough to smash his face in? If anyone would sue you for your coat, get your lawyers on to it immediately and sort him out in the courts. For generosity is a sign of weakness. You have heard it used to be said, "You shall love your neighbour and hate your enemy." But I say unto you, Hate your neighbours also and be suspicious of their intentions. For what good is trust in this day and age? If you love those who love you, you have only yourselves to blame when things turn nasty. Does not everyone do the same? Therefore be selfish, that the whole world might be selfish.'

Judging from Appearances

NARRATOR; NORMAN, *middle-aged church treasurer, some-what set in his ways*; NICK, *a colourful character in charge of the church youth club*

The parables of Jesus are simple and vivid. They make a happy hunting-ground for the biblical sketchwriter but sometimes, because these stories have become so familiar, we miss their original shock impact. When Jesus first told them, they almost always contained an unexpected twist, a sting in the tail, which is there to clarify the deeper issues and explode the prejudice of the audience – a selfish son is welcomed home with open arms, a servant is condemned for being over-cautious, social rejects are the guests of honour at a magnificent banquet. The stories are unforgettable and often highly satirical. Here is a modern treatment of the parable of the Pharisee and the Publican, but who are the latter-day Pharisees? Whom does God accept? Too often we judge only from appearances.

Four chairs are arranged in two rows facing the audience. There is an aisle down the middle. NICK is seated at the front on one side; NORMAN kneels in the second row on the other. The NARRATOR is free to move around them during the introductory speech before taking up a position downstage left where he or she will then administer the bread at communion. It is important that the two actors don't lead the audience to anticipate the twist at the end of the sketch. In the expression of their thoughts before they pray, NORMAN should convey a kind of tense self-righteousness, while NICK should communicate a simple, but thoughtful enthusiasm for what has been happening among the young people in the church. It is as they pray that their true colours are revealed.

NB Without hinting at the twist at the end of the sketch, it should be introduced to the audience as being a modern version of the parable of the Pharisee and the Publican.

NARRATOR: Two men are about to take communion in their local church. Norman Fraser (*Pausing alongside him*), bursar of St Martin's College and treasurer of the church finance committee. And Nick Price, volunteer youth worker and former drug addict. Norman has been a member of the congregation for twenty-six years, during which he has introduced a stewardship scheme and battled hard to make the church heating system more cost-effective. Nick was introduced to the church four years ago by his probation officer. Since his conversion, Nick's lifestyle has changed in some respects. He is no longer involved in armed robbery and drug pushing, but his clothes and record number of tattoos are regarded with suspicion by some members of the congregation. (*Glances at* NORMAN) Listen to the thoughts that occur to these two men in that period of quiet reflection before taking communion.

NORMAN: (*Still kneeling*) I was far from happy with that guest service the other night. I felt the music and the drama were irreverent.

NICK: It's amazing what's happened to me over the last few years. Four years ago I'd have been down the pub right now.

NORMAN: And another thing, the collection was down twenty-five pounds on a normal week. I found that most disappointing. I thought it was typical of the modern attitude.

NICK: (*Surveying the congregation behind him*) It's great the way the youth club's growing. So many have joined since I took over. They can really identify with people like me.

NORMAN: (*Staring straight ahead over the back of the pew*) It's also been worrying me that I cannot identify with the leadership of this church. I haven't liked the new minister, and I have been extremely reluctant to give her my support.

NICK: (*Rising to come forward for communion. As he waits his turn, he stands, looking slightly upwards and prays*) Lord, I really thank you that I became a Christian. I really thank you that I've conquered the past. I'm so happy that

I can give my talents to you and that I can go anywhere and talk to anybody and bring the light of your gospel to all people who feel rejected. I really thank you that you don't have to be hypocritical and wear posh suits and put on posh voices to be a Christian. I really thank you that I'm not like that. Amen. (*He receives communion and then turns upstage to return to his seat by the centre aisle.* NORMAN *gets up. Before leaving his row he says a prayer.* NICK *freezes as he speaks*)

NORMAN: Lord, I'm ashamed of all my attitudes. How can you ever forgive me? (*He moves forward and stands with head bowed to receive the bread.* NICK *moves again to his seat*)

NARRATOR: (*About to hand the bread to* NORMAN) Jesus said, 'I tell you that this man, rather than the other, went home justified before God. For everyone who exalts himself will be humbled and he who humbles himself will be exalted.'

The Lost Sheep

NARRATOR; PHOEBE, *a capable shepherdess*; LAMBERT, *a lovable but independent young sheep*; CHORUS, *a flock of sheep, who behave like a group of rowdy fourth-formers over which the* NARRATOR *is unable to establish full control*

This is a familiar story told in an unfamiliar way by a group of actors, of which the NARRATOR *is the leader. Its effect should be highly theatrical and depends upon great energy, strong chorus interaction, discipline, amusing sound-effects and good timing in order to work properly. The* CHORUS *can be as large as you like. The important thing is that each member of the flock should create his or her own character and be prepared to react in complete harmony with the others. From time to time, individuals may be given occasional lines, but generally the* CHORUS *amplifies the story by acting in unison. They arrange themselves at different levels in a compact group on stage, leaving enough space for the action in front of them. It should be clear from their costume (perhaps pairs of woolly ears?) that they are a flock of sheep.*

This sketch was originally written for performance to children in the context of a family service, but it would also lend itself well to street theatre. A giant cartoon approach is probably best for the creation of the lion: a huge lion-head can be made by holding up the various parts on sticks (the mane, the two eyes and the two jaws) and then choreographing movements to fit the action. 'FX' is a convenient shorthand for the creation of suitable sound-effects by the CHORUS.

NARRATOR: (*He stands in front of his 'class' of sheep and addresses the audience*) Once upon a time there was a flock of sheep. (*With appropriate baas and bleats, the sheep illustrate the various types*) Big ones . . . little ones . . . clever ones . . . and thick ones . . .

posh ones . . . common ones . . . wild ones . . . and woolly ones.

A SHEEP: (*Quavering voice*) Actually, I'm not sure about the Resurrection.

NARRATOR: Some had horns . . . (*Someone makes a silly French horn noise from the back of the group. The* NARRATOR *glares at them*) Give it to me.

SHEEP 1: (*Grumbling*) Ah, *sir.*

NARRATOR: Quickly. (*He confiscates the 'horn'*) But most didn't. (*More surreptitiously, the horn noise comes again*) In all – see me afterwards – there were one hundred sheep. (*He is rattled, but presses on lest the whole situation should get completely out of hand*) They were extremely happy together.

CHORUS: (*Begin to sing the theme from Beethoven's* 'Pastoral' *symphony*)

NARRATOR: It was a wonderful life. The insects hummed,

CHORUS: (*The theme swells briefly with a hum*)

NARRATOR: The birds sang,

CHORUS: (*They sing a few bars loudly to 'la'*)

NARRATOR: And the bees buzzed.

CHORUS: (*They end the theme by 'buzzing' the last few notes very fast*)

NARRATOR: All day long the sheep gambolled

CHORUS: (*Suddenly miming games of poker, etc.*)

NARRATOR: And frisked.

CHORUS: (*They frisk each other for offensive weapons*)

NARRATOR: (*Sternly*) Look! Either we do this seriously or we don't do it at all!

CHORUS: (*Improvise their apologies*)

NARRATOR: Now, in charge of the sheep was a very beautiful young shepherdess called (*Mispronouncing her name*) Phoeeb . . . I'm sorry . . . Phoebe.

CHORUS: (*Wild yodelling of the goatherd song from* The Sound of Music *as* PHOEBE *enters downstage*)

NARRATOR: Yes, thank you. We've all seen it. Many times. She had invented a very good way of getting a lot of sheep into a small space. The sheepfold. First, fold the sheep and then put them into a small space. Ha! Ha! Ha! No, really, she took great care of the sheep. (PHOEBE *mimes the various tasks with different sheep*) She loved them,

CHORUS: (*FX Sentimental Aaaaaahh*)

NARRATOR: She fed them, she watered them, she led them. She removed awkward little stones from their hooves and awkward little stains from their woollens with a regular warm wash

CHORUS: (*FX Washing machine*)

NARRATOR: And spin.

CHORUS: (*FX Action fast spin cycle*)

NARRATOR: Compared with Mrs X, her flocks always came out whiter. Phoebe says:

PHOEBE: This brand always removes marks on my sheep. If I want to do the reverse, I use this brand. (*Mimes seizing red-hot iron*)

CHORUS: (*FX Hiss and shriek as brand is applied to the backside of a sheep*)

NARRATOR: Phoebe knew all her sheep by name.

SHEEP 1:   Baaarney.

SHEEP 2:   Baaarclay.

SHEEP 3:   Baaartholomew.

SHEEP 4:   Baaarbara.

SHEEP 5:   Laaambert.

SHEEP 6:   Eewan.

SHEEP 7:   Raaamsay. (*Pause*)

SHEEP 8:   (*A more tentative offering*) Shorn?

NARRATOR: And many others. They stayed together and they sang together.

PHOEBE: (*Leading the* CHORUS *in singing the nursery rhyme*)
Baa! Baa! Good sheep will together stay,

CHORUS: Yes, Miss. Yes, Miss, if you say.

PHOEBE: Look for the others,
Never, ever stray,

CHORUS: And don't talk to strangers you meet on the way.

PHOEBE: Now, you can all go off and eat.

NARRATOR: (*Smugly to audience*) But do remember to say *graze*. Sorry. Now, the youngest sheep was extremely enthusiastic. (LAMBERT *comes to the front*) He wanted to be everywhere at once and do everything that the older sheep were doing.

LAMBERT: (*Very quickly*) Hey, can I play? Can I play? Can I play? Can I play?

NARRATOR: He had an irritating way of repeating himself.

LAMBERT: What do you mean? What do you mean?

NARRATOR: Oh, never mind.

LAMBERT: (*Eagerly to the other sheep*) Hey, please can I . . .?

CHORUS: Shove off! Get knitted!

LAMBERT: But I want . . .

SHEEP 2: Get lost!

LAMBERT: Why?

SHEEP 8: Because we want to finish the sketch.

LAMBERT: (*As actor*) Oh, fine.

NARRATOR: And so, discouraged and dismissed, he strolled off by himself. Far, far away from the protection of the flock. Higher and higher he climbed.

LAMBERT: I don't need the others!

NARRATOR: He cried, slipping on a patch of wet grass.

LAMBERT: I'm quite happy playing by myself!

NARRATOR: He shouted, scrabbling at the rock face.

LAMBERT: I want to be alone!

NARRATOR: He shrieked, stepping on a loose clod of earth.

LAMBERT: I wish I could fly!

NARRATOR: He commented, reaching the bottom of a ravine. That night the shepherdess counted the sheep.

PHOEBE: One, two, three, four, five, six . . . (*She drifts off to sleep*)

NARRATOR: She never found this easy. (*He wakes* PHOEBE *up*) Eventually, she finished.

PHOEBE: All right! Where's Lambert?

CHORUS: (*Variously*) I dunno. He'll turn up sooner or later. Shouldn't bother about him. Yeah, bit of peace and quiet for a change.

PHOEBE: But you're supposed to look after him! He's only little.

SHEEP 1: Little wally. (*Or other contemporary term of abuse*)

PHOEBE: Why did he run off?

SHEEP 4: 'Cos Baaarclay told him to get lost.

CHORUS: (*Massive groan*) Oooohhh, Baaarclay!

SHEEP 2: (*Who is often persecuted as the form idiot, defensively*) It was only a figure of speech.

PHOEBE: Don't you realise there are lions out there?

CHORUS: L-L-L-Lions!

PHOEBE: And what do lions eat?

SHEEP 3: Lion bars?

PHOEBE: Lambs! You fools!

CHORUS: L-L-L-Lambs!

NARRATOR: So off she ran, leaving the other sheep safely in the fold. There was no time to lose. (PHOEBE *runs round the audience*) She ran through the valley, calling his name.

PHOEBE: Lambert! Lambert! Lambert! (*Fading into the distance*)

NARRATOR: Meanwhile, in the ravine, Lambert was a sitting duck. (LAMBERT *tries to cover his face with a large, yellow beak*) However, this disguise did not fool the lion.

CHORUS: (*FX Lion roar*)

NARRATOR: (*During this speech, the* CHORUS *create the lion*) He was the meanest, wildest, hungriest lion in the land. He had the longest mane, the biggest eyes and was the fastest jaw in the West.

CHORUS: (*Loud roar*)

NARRATOR: The lion prepared himself for dinner. He covered himself with butter and jumped into the oven. He had a very low IQ. At this moment he saw Lambert and emerged from the oven, roaring ferociously.

CHORUS: Ferociously!

NARRATOR: Lambert shared his deep concern about this situation with the rest of the flock.

LAMBERT: (*Yelling*) Aaaaargghh!

CHORUS: (*Together in a deep voice*) Hello, little lamb.

LAMBERT: Pleased to meet you, Mr Lion.

CHORUS: Meat? Did you say *meat*?

LAMBERT: (*Hastily*) No. I was just thinking what a lovely day it was for a picnic . . . er, *picture*. Taking *pictures*.

CHORUS: (*Working the jaws*) You mean *snaps*?

LAMBERT: No. No, no. I was talking about the weather. I'm roasting . . . er, *resting*, ha, ha, ha . . . er, for a moment in these lovely greens . . . er, green surroundings.

CHORUS: Oh, dear, little lamb, you're all by yourself. What a shame. No pudding.

NARRATOR: Lambert's last moment had come. The lion licked his lips and prepared to leap on Lambert.

PHOEBE: (*Off*) Lambert! Lambert! Lambert! (*Getting louder*)

CHORUS: Whassat?

PHOEBE: (*Entering, she sees* LAMBERT) Lambert!

CHORUS: Oh, good. Pudding!

PHOEBE: Not so fast, Pusscat! (*She does a lightning change of costume* à la *Wonder Woman*)

CHORUS: Oh, no! Not Shepherd 'S'!

NARRATOR: She gave him a friendly wave. (PHOEBE *thumps lion between the eyes*)

CHORUS: (*Grunt*)

NARRATOR: Showed him the way out. (PHOEBE *gives the lion a kung fu kick in the jaw*) and finally they parted company. (*The lion falls apart*)

CHORUS: (*Led by* LAMBERT, *FX Cheer!*)

NARRATOR: Lambert and the shepherdess were joyfully reunited. She picked him up, tucked him under her arm and, leaping lightly from crag to crag, she skipped over twenty-five miles back to the fold and was instantly selected for Hull Kingston Rovers.

CHORUS: (*Applause*)

NARRATOR: So there they were, back in the fold, to the great delight of all the other sheep.

CHORUS: (*Feebly*) Hooray.

NARRATOR: Now, come on, I want to hear a proper cheer from everyone.

CHORUS: (*Still without any enthusiasm*) Hooray!

NARRATOR: Unless I hear a proper cheer, this whole sketch is in detention!

CHORUS: (*Wildly*) HOORAAAY!

NARRATOR: All right, settle down. Now, what's the point of the story? Lambert?

LAMBERT: I was lost but now I'm found.

NARRATOR: Good. Phoebe?

PHOEBE: I rejoice more in finding one lost sheep than I do over all the ninety-nine who stayed at home.

NARRATOR: Excellent. Sheep?

CHORUS: Umm . . . errr . . .

NARRATOR: (*Wearily*) Oh, never mind. Just read the words on the card. (*He holds up placard*)

CHORUS: The Lord is my Shepherd, He gives me everything I need, For ever and ever. Baa-aa-men.

Albert Mayhem's Automania

NARRATOR; CHORUS (*five or more actors*); ALBERT MAYHEM, *a car manufacturer*

This sketch is based on the parable Jesus told of the Workers in the Vineyard. It continues the group story-telling formula used in other pieces such as 'David and Goliath' or 'The Lost Sheep'. Although there are individual characters who emerge from the CHORUS *from time to time, the overall feel should be of the whole group collaborating vocally and physically to tell the story. The central image is of a car factory. Skill and ingenuity will be required to develop the standard theatre workshop idea of 'building a machine', into the detailed sounds and movements of a production line. This vigorous activity is accompanied by a strong, two-beat, vocal rhythm, which is then echoed by the action and text in the various places from which the workers are recruited. Above all, the sketch requires disciplined choreography and great energy.*

NARRATOR: What is the Kingdom of Heaven like?

VOICES: It's like . . . It's like . . . er . . . It's like . . . I dunno, give us a clue. Etc.

NARRATOR: Somewhere where they make travel goods.

VOICES: Debenham's? Marks and Spencer's? Hong Kong?

NARRATOR: Goods you can travel in.

VOICE 1: Aha! I know. Cars.

NARRATOR: Correct. A car plant.

VOICE 2: What's a car plant?

VOICE 3: One that flowers at seventy miles an hour!

NARRATOR: (*Sarcastic*) Thank you. Yes, the Kingdom of Heaven is like a car factory in the middle of a recession.

CHORUS: A car factory in the middle of a recession???

NARRATOR: A crazy car factory that refused to stop production.

CHORUS: (*The actors create the mechanical movement and*

sound effects of one stage of a car production line, chanting to a solid rhythm)
Building and Working. Building and Working. Building and Working. Building and Working.

NARRATOR: Great cars! (*The actors mime driving a great car*) Family cars! (*The car is now full of kids and harassed parents*) Cars that everyone could afford! (*The actors roar away in their separate vehicles, leaving the* NARRATOR *coughing in a cloud of exhaust fumes*)

CHORUS: (*Singing well-known advert*) Take my breath away . . .

VOICE: (*Waving at the* NARRATOR) Papa!

NARRATOR: (*Still choking*) Nicole!

VOICE 4: Mile after mile of trouble-free motoring!

VOICES: Just put petrol in your tank and go! Go! GO!!

ALBERT: (*Expansively*) Welcome to Albert Mayhem's Automania!!

CHORUS: (*The second stage of the production line begins; chanting to the same rhythm*) Bolting and Fixing. Bolting and Fixing. Bolting and Fixing. Bolting and Fixing.

NARRATOR: As the recession began to bite, soon Albert Mayhem's Automania was the only factory still –

CHORUS: Building and Working. Building and Working. Etc.

NARRATOR: Business was booming. The phones never stopped ringing. (*Actors are going mental trying to answer eight phones each*) The fax machines went crazy! (*FX*) Orders came flooding in from Germany . . .

VOICE 1: (*Strong German accent*) Halt! Get back in line!!

NARRATOR: From Japan . . .

CHORUS: (*Bowing politely on each name*) Nissan. Honda. Toyota.

VOICE 3: (*Sneezing*) Mitsubishi!

NARRATOR: Bless you . . . Even from Mrs Posselthwaite at number 23.

VOICE 5: I'll have a plain one, please, duck.

NARRATOR: Early one morning, Albert Mayhem woke with a start. (*He is 'started' by a cord-pull from an outboard motor*) Took a cool look at his situation. (*Says 'Hi' to himself in the mirror*) And nipped down to the local Job

Centre before the doors were open. (*The actors are a group of job-seekers, studying adverts, making notes, hanging about*)

CHORUS: (*Moving mechanically and chanting*) Peering and Checking. Hoping for Something. Nothing to be Doing.

NARRATOR: The only vacancies were for honest politicians and skilled shepherds with over ten years' experience.

ALBERT: Listen, everybody! I've got jobs for vacant car workers!

CHORUS: Eh?

ALBERT: No, I haven't. I've got vacancies for jobbing car workers!

CHORUS: Eh?

ALBERT: Oh, look. Can you use a spanner?

VOICE 2: Eh?

ALBERT: Get yourselves down to Albert Mayhem's Automania and get spannering. I'll pay you what's right.

VOICE 3: Just a minute! Just a minute! (*The actors have a quick huddled meeting*) As representative of the newly-formed committee of the Transport and General Workers' Union, I must point out in the interests of my members that we won't settle for anything less than full union rates: six pound fifty per hour with strict adherence in respect of tea-break, dinner-break, leg-break, off-break, sanitary and hygiene break.

VOICE 4: Yer wot?

VOICE 5: Going to the lavvy, lovey.

ALBERT: Fine! I'll pay all of you over the minimum rate for a good day's work – fifty-six pounds.

VOICE 4: Wow! You're on!

VOICE 3: Hang on! Hang on! That's no way to conduct negotiations. We have to go away and give due consideration to the man's proposal, returning with an advantageous counter-proposal. (*Pause*) We'll do it!

NARRATOR: Immediately they clocked on (*FX*) and set to work.

CHORUS: (*Creating another stage of the production line, chanting aggressively*) Welding and Clamping. Welding and Clamping. Welding and Clamping. Welding and Clamping.

NARRATOR: At the first tea-break, Albert Mayhem had a brilliant idea.

ALBERT: (*Yelling*) TEA-BREAK!!

NARRATOR: He shouted.

ALBERT: I've had a brilliant idea! Why am I using all these machines? I could get a person to do that. And that.

NARRATOR: So he sprinted off to the Dole Office, where people were –

CHORUS: (*In a queue, advancing towards an official*) Waiting and Queueing. Hoping for Something. Mounting Frustration. Gissa Job, Mate!!

ALBERT: (*Intervening quickly*) Hey! Get yourselves down to Albert Mayhem's Automania and you can do the rest of the day.

VOICE 2:   Well, if I took a job with you, it'd mean I couldn't sign on, could I? I'd lose my dole.

ALBERT: I'll make it worth your while, Missus.

NARRATOR: Workers were clocking on in droves. (*Clocking on FX*)

CHORUS: (*Another energetic section of the production line, with FX and chanting*) Riveting and Bonding. Riveting and Bonding. Riveting and Bonding. Riveting and Bonding.

NARRATOR: Cars were rocketing out of the factory. (*FX of firework rockets shooting into the sky, followed by 'Ooohs' and 'Aaahs'*) The order book was bursting. (*Someone has neglected to visit the bathroom*) Production soared. (*Silly sawing FX*) At dinner-time, Albert Mayhem expanded his workforce again. (*Huge stomachs appear suddenly*) He belted off down the High Street to where everybody was –

CHORUS: (*In positions of studied inactivity*) Sitting or Standing. Loafing and Dossing. Hoping for Something.

ALBERT: Oi, you lot! Hop down to my car plant and get yourselves a few bob!

VOICES: Hey, Bob! Come on, Bob! What's that, Bob? Got yourself a job, Bob? OK, Bob. Sounds good to me, Bob. You coming, Bob? Etc.

NARRATOR: So, (*Pleased with this witticism*) from a production line full of robots, Albert now had one packed full of Roberts!

CHORUS: (*General groans and encouragement to get on with it, etc. They create another action-packed phase of the production line, chanting*) Wiring and Sparking. Wiring and Sparking. Wiring and Sparking.

NARRATOR: Come tea time, Albert Mayhem popped into his local for a quiet pint.

CHORUS: (*Immediately create a rowdy pub scene*)

NARRATOR: I said a quiet pint! Suddenly, it struck him! This pub was full of people –

CHORUS: (*In strict rhythm with actions*) Sipping and Smoking. Yakking and Swearing.

ALBERT: Hey, hey, hey! We can't have all this –

CHORUS: Sipping and Smoking. Yakking and Swearing.

ALBERT: There's still time to start painting and spraying down at the works. I'll pay you what's right. There's at least half an hour to go.

CHORUS: (*Creating the sights and sounds of the paint shop*) Painting and Spraying. Coating and Squirting. Painting and Spraying. Coating and Squirting.

NARRATOR: With only half an hour of the working day left, Albert Mayhem was back down to the Job Centre.

CHORUS: (*Forming another group of hopeful workers*) Peering and Checking. Hoping for Something.

NARRATOR: His generous heart beat faster and faster.

ALBERT: Get yourselves clocked on, lads! It's better than going home empty-handed.

CHORUS: (*Creating the final stage of the production line*) Polishing and Finishing. Polishing and Finishing. Etc.

NARRATOR: The factory was buzzing right up to the final hooter for the end of the day. (*FX*) Hundreds of gleaming cars lined the car park, as the workers lined up for their wages.

VOICE 4:   The Assistant Manager, Beryl Budget, that's me, dealt with the payments on Albert's instructions.

(*Each actor approaches her*)

VOICE 5:   I've only worked since half past four.

VOICE 4:   There you are, then.

VOICE 2:   I came at three o'clock.

VOICE 4:   That's yours.

VOICE 3:   Dinner-time.

VOICE 5:   (*Examining pay packet*) Hey! Look at that! What have you got?

VOICE 2:   Fifty-six quid!

VOICE 5:   So have I!

VOICE 1:   (*To Beryl*) I've been here since first thing.

VOICE 4:   There you are. I think you'll find that's all present and correct.

NARRATOR: When all the workers had checked their pay, (*FX rapid riffling through money*) there was a short silence.

VOICE 1:   (*Checking his watch*) Right, that's enough of that. What's going on here?

NARRATOR: A rumbling on the shop floor.

CHORUS: Grumbling and Stirring. Grumbling and Stirring.

VOICE 1:   We've worked since eight o'clock this morning!

CHORUS: (*Continuing to build the atmosphere of discontent*)

NARRATOR: (*Coming forward and attempting vainly to end the sketch on a happy note*) So, you see, the Kingdom of Heaven is like a great, big, happy car factory . . . one happy family, really, in the middle of a recession . . .

VOICE 1:   (*Interrupting*) Excuse me! Excuse me! There's a problem here. A problem of industrial relations.

CHORUS: WE WANT JUSTICE! ALBERT, ALBERT, ALBERT! OUT! OUT! OUT!

NARRATOR: So Albert came out.

ALBERT: Now then, now then! What's all this?

VOICE 2:   We've been sweating away in your flaming factory since first thing this morning. And we've only got fifty-six quid to show for it.

ALBERT: I'm sorry. Is something wrong? What did we agree?

VOICE 1:   Fifty-six pounds.

ALBERT: And how much have you got?

VOICE 1:   That's just the problem – only fifty-six pounds!

VOICE 3:   Same as them who've been flicking a feather duster for half an hour.

ALBERT: Well, that should cheer them up. 'Spread a little happiness around' and all that. Now listen. You've got what you came for. If I choose to put a smile on the faces of them who didn't think they'd get a job at all, that's my business.

That's Albert Mayhem's Automania for you. Now, you take your money home and think about it. I'll expect you back at eight o'clock sharp tomorrow morning.

NARRATOR: And that is why

VOICE 4:   The Kingdom of Heaven

VOICE 3:   Is like a crazy car factory

VOICE 1:   Where everyone can work

VOICE 5:   For the same reward

NARRATOR: As soon as they clock on.

CHORUS: (*Creating a final image of synchronised motion*) Building and Working. Building and Working. (*All freeze in mid-action*)

The Last Judgement

THE VOICE OF CHRIST; DAVE, *a man relaxing at home*; CONNIE, *a cleaner*; MYRTLE, *a cleaner*

Because of its simplicity this sketch will stand on its own and will provoke thought in virtually any situation. Choosing the best context for it, however, needs great care. Anything on the subject of judgement, particularly judgement after death, will stir up strong feelings and it may be best to perform the piece as part of a talk. The vast majority of the sketches in this anthology have an atmosphere of celebration. This sketch is a reminder of some of the harder sayings in the gospels and has been preserved, despite its bluntness, because of the number of people who have written to us over the years, commenting favourably about its impact on their lives.

Centre stage there is a large free-standing door, facing the audience. In front of this is an armchair in which DAVE *is sitting, reading the paper.*

VOICE OF CHRIST: Listen. I stand at the door and knock. If anyone hears my voice and opens the door, I will come into his house and eat with him and he will eat with me. (*Knocking*)

DAVE: Can't get any peace even to read the paper these days, can yer? Who is it, anyway?

VOICE OF CHRIST: The person you've been waiting for.

DAVE: I haven't been waiting for anybody, mate.

VOICE OF CHRIST: Can I come in?

DAVE: What do you mean, 'can I come in?' This is my home. You can't just come in here. I didn't invite you. (*He continues to read the paper. Pause. The knocking begins again*) Push off, will yer? Some people won't take no for an answer, will they? (*He gets up and goes across to the door*) Look, mate, I don't want to seem unfriendly . . . if there's anything you want . . .

VOICE OF CHRIST: I want to come in.

DAVE: Well, you can't. I'm busy. Try again when I've got more time. Try Wednesday. (*He sits down and reads. Silence. More knocking*) This is ridiculous. How many times do I have to tell yer? (*He gets up and goes back to the door*) Look, let's be reasonable. I'm really interested in what you've got to say. A lot of people wouldn't even talk to you, would they? But I'm not like that. No, I've read your book . . . well, some of it. But look. I'm busy and I'm tired, the wife's busy and she's tired, the dog's busy and he's tired – we're all tired in here, all right? I'd love to chat for longer, but it'll have to wait, okay?

(*He sits down again and reads. The knocking continues, but each knock is like ten years of his life passing. In slow motion, following the softer and softer beats on the door, he becomes an old man*)

I'm tired. (*He collapses on to the floor*)

(*Enter* CONNIE *and* MYRTLE)

MYRTLE: You start up the stairs, Connie, and I'll do the floor. All right, love?

CONNIE: (*Seeing the body*) 'Ere, Myrtle, come and look at this.

MYRTLE: Ooh my goodness me. 'Ow long's 'e been 'ere?

CONNIE: Day or so.

MYRTLE: Still, 'e was gettin' on.

CONNIE: Come on, let's go and get the police. I can't stand lookin' at bodies.

MYRTLE: Makes yer think though.

CONNIE: What?

MYRTLE: Well, I always wonder where people go when they die.

(*Exeunt. Dave slowly stirs from where he has been lying. He looks around him, bewildered. He sees the door, walks up to it and starts to knock*)

DAVE: Hallo? Hallo? Anyone in? It's me . . . David. Dave. Come on, you remember me, Davey? Hey, can I come in? (*Silence*) We met before. At my place. We had a chat. Remember? I talked to you. You were going to come round sometime. You were going to come back . . . on Wednesday, that was it. Remember? I said you could come back. I said you could . . . (*He hammers on the door*)

VOICE OF CHRIST: Who are you?

DAVE: Dave. You remember me.

VOICE OF CHRIST: (*With great sadness*) I never knew you. (DAVE *freezes in front of the door, facing audience*)

The Appointment

SECRETARY; BUSINESSMAN; JESUS

This is a very simple sketch, based on the encounter between Jesus and the Rich Young Ruler. The character of the BUSINESSMAN *is not identical to that of his Biblical counterpart but the challenge to him is the same. 'Up-dating' stories is simple to do and can be very necessary for church audiences over-familiar with the text. It can also be a revelation, despite apparent incongruity, to see Jesus speaking in a familiar twentieth-century situation. It should also be said that a straightforward conversation piece like this, which is 'low-key' dramatically, is sometimes the most appropriate form for dovetailing into a service.*

A SECRETARY *is seated at an office desk, with papers, word processor and telephone. Enter a stylishly dressed* BUSINESSMAN.

BUSINESSMAN: Morning, Freda.

SECRETARY: Good morning, Mr Stevenson – here are some things for you to sign.

BUSINESSMAN: Look, I'm a bit pushed this morning, I've got this religious fellow coming to see me in a few minutes. What are they? Anything important?

SECRETARY: Well, there are those two big contracts you concluded yesterday with ICI and Lever Brothers and that cheque for five thousand pounds for the Indian Cyclone disaster.

BUSINESSMAN: Oh yes, and what about the Mercedes I saw yesterday, did you order it?

SECRETARY: Yes.

BUSINESSMAN: I must have it by the board meeting at the end of the month.

SECRETARY: In Brussels?

BUSINESSMAN: No, Paris, then Brussels. Any phone calls this morning?

SECRETARY: One about some investments in Computer Services International and one from Miss Silversmith.

BUSINESSMAN: Miss Silversmith?

SECRETARY: Your fiancée.

BUSINESSMAN: Oh yes.

SECRETARY: She was suggesting dinner with her parents next Friday.

BUSINESSMAN: Oh dear, was she? Well, am I free?

SECRETARY: (*Flipping through diary*) No.

BUSINESSMAN: Good. Will you ring her back, then? Is that all?

SECRETARY: Yes.

BUSINESSMAN: Righto, thanks, Freda.

(*She goes, showing* JESUS *into the office on her way out*) Ah, hello. I'm really pleased and honoured to have you come to my office. (*They shake hands*)

JESUS: I've been looking forward to meeting you.

BUSINESSMAN: I hope you won't mind me asking you one or two questions that have been on my mind recently. You've got such a reputation for being a good counsellor and I'd value some advice.

JESUS: Why do you call me good? No one is good except God.

(*Silence. The* BUSINESSMAN *averts his eyes from* JESUS)

BUSINESSMAN: Hmmm. What I'm really interested in is . . . well, you must realise that a man in my position stands to lose a lot if I should . . . well, er, *die* really. And so what I'm asking is, is there any way I can be sure that I'm not going to lose everything . . . that I can have what you call Eternal Life?

JESUS: You know the commandments?

BUSINESSMAN: Yes.

JESUS: Do not commit adultery . . .

BUSINESSMAN: Couldn't agree more. I'm not married of course . . . yet, but . . .

JESUS: Do not murder, do not steal.

BUSINESSMAN: Quite, absolutely.

JESUS: Do not tell lies.
   (*Pause*)
BUSINESSMAN: Uh-huh.
JESUS: Honour your father and mother.
BUSINESSMAN: Yes, dear old things. Well, yes, I've lived
   my life along these sort of lines since I was a kid. I'd even
   go so far as to say it's been a very moral life. But all
   that seems rather easy, really, when one's talking about
   Eternal Life. A bit cheap, if you see what I mean. (*Pause*)
   Is that all there is to it?
   (*Silence.* JESUS *looks at him*)
JESUS: What is the most important thing in your life?
BUSINESSMAN: Well, that's hard to say, I suppose . . .
JESUS: Who has first place in your life?
BUSINESSMAN: My fiancée, I should think . . .
JESUS: Where does your security lie? In your bank
   balance?
BUSINESSMAN: Look, aren't we getting a bit off the sub-
   ject here? I'm asking you about Eternal Life and you're
   just dodging the issue . . . it seems to me . . . sir.
JESUS: Is that what you really want?
BUSINESSMAN: Eternal Life? Yes, I suppose so. It's not
   the sort of thing you can buy, though, is it? (*He gives an
   embarrassed laugh*)
JESUS: You don't have to. Just come now and follow me.
   Obey me and share my life. (*Pause*) Are you free enough
   to do that?
BUSINESSMAN: Of course I'm free. I can do whatever I
   like.
JESUS: (*Gently*) Fine.
BUSINESSMAN: What do you mean, 'fine'?
JESUS: Well, sell all your possessions, give the money to
   the poor and come and follow me. (*Silence*) What's wrong?
BUSINESSMAN: You can't be serious?
JESUS: For you, this is the most important thing.
BUSINESSMAN: I couldn't do that.
   (JESUS *leaves slowly*)
   I couldn't possibly do that . . . I couldn't do that . . . I
   couldn't do that . . .

For the Good of the Team
by Nigel Forde

CAIAPHAS, *a football trainer, weak, worried but aggressive*;
PILATE, *a football chairman, powerful, needs success*

*Like all sketches which say one thing in terms of another, this
sketch treads a delicate tightrope between illumination and
obscurity. It is deceptively easy and needs careful direction;
but if it is acted with real conviction and not allowed to fall
into caricature it can be quite chilling. It is extremely important
that the first four words be clearly heard!*

CAIAPHAS *enters; he is slightly nervous. Despite his ambition
and determination he is never quite sure of how to handle
PILATE. He does a few casual warm-up movements to calm
his nerves, but stops immediately* PILATE *enters.* PILATE *comes
in swiftly. Sun-glasses, big tie, coat collar up. He possesses the
stage. The rest of the movement in the sketch belongs almost
entirely to* CAIAPHAS.

PILATE: Morning, Caiaphas.
CAIAPHAS: Morning, Pilate.
PILATE: I hope you've got something important to say. I've
a lot of work on. Where are the others?
CAIAPHAS: It's . . . um . . . it's just you and me, sir.
PILATE: (*Patronisingly*) I'm intrigued.
CAIAPHAS: A bit of trouble with the team.
PILATE: I thought it was doing very well.
CAIAPHAS: (*Quickly, to preclude criticism*) Ah, yes! In a
manner of speaking, it is. Yes.
PILATE: (*Patiently*) Well then?
CAIAPHAS: (*Not quite knowing how to begin*) Well, sir . . . a
team, you see sir . . . it's . . . well, it's a team, isn't it?
PILATE: Devastating, Caiaphas.
CAIAPHAS: I mean, you can't have someone in a team

who's . . . who's different. I expect you know who I'm
talking about.

PILATE: I could hazard a guess. From what I hear he is
very good.

CAIAPHAS: (*Playing for time*) Well, it all depends on . . .

PILATE: He's original.

CAIAPHAS: (*Grudgingly*) Oh, yeah, well I suppose . . .

PILATE: Creative, unselfish.

CAIAPHAS: (*Still unwilling to concede a point*) Yes, you could
say . . .

PILATE: He inspires the rest of the team and he gets results.
What's wrong with that?

CAIAPHAS: (*Suddenly savage*) He doesn't play it by the
book!

PILATE: (*Quickly*) Fouls?

CAIAPHAS: Well, no; not exactly fouls, no. But he doesn't
play the way I want the team to play. Look, this team has
got a history, a tradition to live up to . . .

PILATE: And that doesn't include doing well . . .?

CAIAPHAS: (*Firmly*) No! (*Suddenly realising what he has said*)
I mean yes! I mean . . .

PILATE: You mean he is just too good for you. He knows
more about the game than you do and you don't like
it.

CAIAPHAS: The rest of the team can't live up to him. Look,
I've got to train them, haven't I? That's my job. How can
I tell them one thing when he goes out there and does
something entirely different?

PILATE: And gets results. Look, the fans love him, don't
they?

CAIAPHAS: (*Disgusted*) Oh, the fans, the fans; what do they
matter? (*Ingratiatingly*) I'm thinking of the team. Individual
skills are all very well, but it's teamwork that counts. He
shows everybody up; he's got to go!

PILATE: (*Putting* CAIAPHAS *in his place*) And you're going to
get rid of him.

CAIAPHAS: (*Laughing off his embarrassment*) Ah . . . no, well
. . . you see, I can't. Can I? *You* can, being on the board
and that . . .

PILATE: Which is why I am here. (*Bringing the conversation to a close*) Well, I don't see the problem. I can't fault him.

CAIAPHAS: (*Quietly, almost casually*) He's, er . . . he's after the boss's job, of course.

PILATE: (*Suddenly alert. Urgently*) He's what?

CAIAPHAS: Stands to reason, dunnit? He's going to cause a division. It's his style or the boss's style. (*He feels that at last he has the upper hand and spells it out quietly and deliberately*) Loyalties will change.

PILATE: (*Without admitting anything*) So, what do you want me to do? Free transfer?

CAIAPHAS: No, no, no. He'll be a troublemaker wherever he goes; bring the whole game into disrepute.

PILATE: What then?

CAIAPHAS: (*Quietly*) Just . . . er, just suspend him for a while (*pause*) if you get my meaning . . .?

(*They remain motionless as the lights slowly fade*)

The Light of the World

PEOPLE, *four men and two women*; CHRIST; NARRATOR

Although the barest outline of all the sketches published in this book, this piece has probably had the greatest impact. It has derived this from vivid stylisation alongside the simple truths of the gospel. The stage directions can only convey a rough idea of the sketch in performance; it is really presented for your own interpretation and as an example of the use of scripture in dramatic performance.

There have been and will be many different stagings of this sketch. Some of this action described here represents an early performance, but it is not intended to limit your own creativity in devising an interpretation suited to the nature and numbers of your company.

The action of the mime takes place round a ladder. The opening 'frame' is the figure of CHRIST, *standing towards the top of the ladder, but facing away from the audience, whilst the six actors hunch down as low as they can, facing towards the audience (but their faces hidden in their hands). For the first half of the sketch they are in two groups, with one woman to each group – and both these groups are now formed stage left and stage right.*

NARRATOR: No one has seen God.
   (*The two groups come to life, but their hands still shield their eyes, blindfolding them from God*)
   But God became a human being and lived among us.
   (CHRIST *turns and faces the audience*)
   He was full of truth and light.
   (*As he descends the ladder*)
   The light has come into the world, but men loved the darkness rather than the light because they do evil things.

(The PEOPLE *are stung by the presence of the light and retreat into their groups, occupying themselves with evil)*

And anyone who does evil things hates the pure light and will not come to the light, because he doesn't want his evil deeds to be shown up.

(Lovingly, CHRIST *attempts to make contact but he is repelled by the* PEOPLE, *who freeze into positions of perverse delight in evil and protection of their lives from the influence of* CHRIST. *In the stillness,* CHRIST *stretches out his hands, as if to shine in the world despite the unresponsiveness of human hearts. As he does this, the* NARRATOR *says)*

The light shines in the darkness of the evil of men's hearts – where the trouble begins.

(A drum begins to beat, simulating the human heart. As the NARRATOR *says the next line, the* PEOPLE *relax into neutral positions)*

Out of the heart of every man comes: *(The catalogue of sins are presented like a series of ten snapshots; they should be carefully worked on for the maximum uniqueness of each pose. Freeze each time long enough for the audience to take the image into account. Throughout this, the 'heart' continues beating)*

Evil thoughts

Lust

Murder

Adultery

Deceit

Envy

Scandalmongering

Pride

Foolishness

Violence

(During this sequence, CHRIST *has faced away and is lashed by each sin as if he were being flogged before the crucifixion. As the* NARRATOR *says the following line, the groups relax the last pose and stand in a crescent from stage right to stage left, with the central actors slightly nearer the audience)*

This is why the heart of man must be changed –

Not the world

(The actors point out to the world around them, as a single movement starting with the actor standing farthest stage left, and moving through the group like a wave)

Not history

(Any suitable positions, e.g. reading books, digging up archaeological remains)

Not governments

(Each actor stamps his foot and raises his right hand in salute)

Not the economic situation

(Everyone is penniless)

Not the newspaper headlines

(Some read newspapers, others mime newsvending)

Not the man next door

(Everyone points to someone else)

Not your wife

(The men point to the women)

Your husband

(The women point to the men)

But you – you – you – you – you.

(On each 'you' the actors point to different people, first to one another, then to different parts of the audience, and on the final 'you' they all shout it with the NARRATOR *as they swing round and point to* CHRIST. *Stamping their feet, and hammering their fists into the air, they close in on* CHRIST *and beat him back up the ladder. They crucify him, the accelerating drum beats suddenly becoming the hammer blows of nails into his hands. Exhausted, they all drop down to the foot of the ladder, heads bowed as* CHRIST *hangs on the cross. His head drops forward as he dies. There is silence. Music, if available, can be played softly – perhaps the best is a human voice singing a lament very quietly, but there should be nothing forced or sentimental. Gradually, two of the men raise their heads, then stand to take* CHRIST *down from the cross. They lower his body to the ground, and turn away upstage. The* NARRATOR *speaks)*

Your life must be changed. You must start all over again. And this is possible because Jesus, who was perfect, died in our place. He paid the penalty for the evil in our hearts so that we might live. He gave the light for the darkness. (*At this*, CHRIST *gets up and steps forward*)

The light shines in the darkness and the darkness has never put it out.

(CHRIST *turns away from the audience towards the* PEOPLE, *who are still standing and kneeling behind him. It is as if he has suddenly appeared in the upper room. Sensing movement behind them, the* PEOPLE *turn round sharply and stare at the risen* CHRIST. *Their faces show a range of emotions: fear, amazement and joy*)

The Newcomer

LUMINOUS, *an angel;* CUMULUS, *an angel;* THIEF

In all the agony and sorrow of the accounts of the death of Jesus, there is one incident which brings a shaft of joy into the narrative. Jesus turns to a dying thief being crucified alongside him and says, 'Today you will be with me in Paradise.' Suddenly we understand something of what the death of Jesus can mean to each of us. The thief's redemption is tangible proof of the gospel of grace: that those who are dying for their sins, who cannot possibly earn their own forgiveness, can still be saved by the mercy of God. Even though his earthly life has only a few hours to run, from the moment he acknowledges Jesus as king, the thief enters that eternal kingdom by the grace of God. For him, the gates of Paradise are unlocked at the eleventh hour. This sketch imagines what happened next.

LUMINOUS *and* CUMULUS *are on duty at the gates of Heaven. Care should be taken over their appearance as angels. It may be best to leave their 'angel-ness' to the audience's imagination, or to find an image which evokes the idea of servants or even 'saints' humbly going about their duties in Heaven. Recent Riding Lights productions have tried to reflect in a serious way, through subtle use of accents, the fact that Heaven is obviously filled with those who have died in faith from all over the world.*

CUMULUS: Exciting, isn't it?
LUMINOUS: Being on the gates of Heaven? Yes, very.
CUMULUS: Your first time, is it?
LUMINOUS: First time, yes. And you?
CUMULUS: Me? Oh, yes. First time.
  (*Pause*)
LUMINOUS: Got the book, then?
CUMULUS: I thought you had it?

LUMINOUS: Oh, silly me, so I have. First night nerves. Sorry.

CUMULUS: Who do you think it's going to be? Maybe a Roman emperor or a king or a famous poet!

LUMINOUS: Possibly. It's certainly going to be somebody mighty special.

CUMULUS: Just think – the first person to arrive in Paradise after the gates have been thrown open. What a privilege! (*A* THIEF, *bloodstained, ragged, unwashed bursts on to the stage. He gazes all around, amazed*)

THIEF: 'E weren't jokin' neither!

(*The* ANGELS *exchange glances*)

LUMINOUS: Sorry, sir?

THIEF: 'E weren't joking' about 'is kingdom an' that!

CUMULUS: I beg your pardon?

THIEF: This is Paradise, innit, Guv?

CUMULUS: Yes.

(*The* ANGELS *cough nervously*)

THIEF: Terrific, eh?

LUMINOUS: Er . . . we like it, sir.

THIEF: Like it! Do us a favour, this is fantastic! Look at them trees towerin' like a thousand feet high, wiv every leaf shimmerin' like a gold bar an' all that stuff. (*There is an uneasy pause.* LUMINOUS *shuffles through his papers, then looks up*)

LUMINOUS: Do you have any credentials, sir?

THIEF: Wot?

LUMINOUS: Papers? Identification? A certificate of approval?

THIEF: Gorra copy of me death warrant. Any good?

LUMINOUS: I – I think there's been some mistake.

CUMULUS: What my colleague means is, er, what have you *done* in your life that might give you entrance to . . .?

THIEF: Done? You mean done in?

CUMULUS: I'm sorry?

THIEF: Done in. I mean, I've done in a few people, worked 'em over. Done a bit of blag, y'know, a few good earners, robberies wiv violence, GBH. Yeah, I been around in my time, but never seen no place like this.

(LUMINOUS *takes* CUMULUS *aside. He talks urgently*)

LUMINOUS: Who is responsible for the Admissions Policy?

CUMULUS: I don't know. But, *technically* the doors are now wide open.

LUMINOUS: Not that wide! Now we've got a gate-crasher at the banquet!

THIEF: Look at them flowers like diamonds! I tell yer, if I'd known about this place and seen all this gear, I wouldn't 'ave bothered wiv that job on Pontius Pilate's country residence. No way, I'd 'ave been up 'ere and ripped this place off. And yet – funny, innit – all them lovely things an' that, an' I 'aven't put one in me pocket. I ask yer, me! Ron the Con. It's a laugh, innit?

CUMULUS: What did you say your name was?

THIEF: Ron the Con. Get it?

CUMULUS: Sorry?

THIEF: Yeah, told yer, I done me fair share, then I got pulled in. Well, I didn't know it were Pontius' joint, did I? Course, it were crawlin' wiv Roman filth, weren't it? The whole bleedin' ninth legion, no less, so I got me collar felt.

LUMINOUS: You had what?

THIEF: Are you deaf or sunninck? I was sussed, weren't I? Wiv the bung in me 'and, the jewels an' that – wiv me dagger still fresh from the job, drippin' wiv blood all over the shop.

CUMULUS: You killed someone with your dagger?

THIEF: Well, I didn't tickle 'im under the chin, did I? What's up wiv you lot?

LUMINOUS: (*Panicking*) I'm sorry. There's been a dreadful administrative error.

CUMULUS: Impossible. Heavenly beings do not make errors.

LUMINOUS: Lucifer made a pretty big one.

CUMULUS: Well, maybe there are things which even arch-angels do not understand yet – maybe –

LUMINOUS: You're not trying to tell me that all these trumpets and hallelujahs and all this rejoicing all over the place are for the benefit of a fouth-mouthed common criminal! I just don't believe this. I'm going to the top to get official verification. (*Exit*)

CUMULUS: Don't leave me on my own, he might be dangerous! (*Turns round nervously and bumps into* THIEF. *Jumps*) Ah, still here, are you?

THIEF: Yeah, I thought I'd 'ave a look round.

CUMULUS: Oh well, that's nice. Good. Um. May I ask who sent you here?

THIEF: Funny you should ask that. I don't know 'is name, actually. I think it was something beginnin' wiv J. He were on the cross next to me.

CUMULUS: (*Suddenly realises. Awed*) You mean – the Lamb of God, the Holy One, the Prince of Peace!

THIEF: No, not any of those, it was – Jesus, that's it. That was the feller's name. (CUMULUS *bows low in adoration of Christ*) 'Ere, what's up wiv you, got stomach cramp or sunninck? Jesus! Yeah, that was 'is name . . . Jesus . . . There we were both dyin', only me for me crimes an' that, caught at it – got me deserts – but 'im, what 'ad 'e done? Nothing. I could see that, couldn't I? Do us a favour. I thought, what's a poor Charlie like that wind up on Death Row for? Then I knew – 'e were no ordinary geezer. There was something about 'im. Fear. I saw it – not in 'im, no! – in *them*, religious leaders an' that. They were in a right funk, weren't they? Knees knockin'! I saw their game – they were standing around watchin' to check 'e didn't leap off. I kid you not! Now who ever leapt off a cross, eh? Give us a break. Different 'e were, talkin' about 'is kingdom! Mumblin', people weepin', holdin' on to 'is feet an' 'im talking about comin' into 'is kingdom! I said, 'Listen, mate, remember me when you get into that kingdom.' Then 'e looked at me, you never seen nothin' like them eyes – lookin', searchin', probin' into me soul. An' then he speaks to me – straight out, bang to rights – he says, 'This day you shall be wiv me in Paradise.' (*Pause*) That were the nicest thing anyone had said to me all day. 'Paradise?' I says, 'Where the hell's Paradise?' I says. An 'e said nothin'. 'E smiled. In that agony 'e smiled. I didn't know where Paradise were an' that, but if 'e were gonna be there, I wanted to be in on the act, know what I mean? (LUMINOUS *rushes back and seizes* CUMULUS *by the arm*)

LUMINOUS: This is really embarrassing!

CUMULUS: (*Still spellbound*) I know.

LUMINOUS: We've committed a terrible *faux pas*!

CUMULUS: I know. Isn't it wonderful?

LUMINOUS: Wonderful! I've just gone and made a fool of myself with the Archangel Gabriel! I said, 'There's been a dreadful mistake, this man's a common criminal, he's nobody special at all!' And Gabriel said, 'Well, he is now.' Then he said, 'What's your definition of special?' And before I had time to reply, he said he thought 'a personal invitation to Paradise from the Lord of Life made a person quite special enough, thank you very much'. Then all the seraphim laughed their heads off. I tell you, if cherubs could blush, I would have gone golden. (*Turning to the* THIEF) Your Grace, I really do apologise for any inconvenience that my vacillations may have caused.

THIEF: Wot?

LUMINOUS: (*Producing magnificent robes*) Please try this for size.

THIEF: 'Ere, what's all the fab gear for then, eh?

LUMINOUS: (*As both* ANGELS *dress* THIEF) The banquet. You're the guest of honour.

THIEF: Somebody's birthday, is it?

LUMINOUS: Yes, yours. Incredible isn't it? The last person shall be the first, and the first shall be last!

CUMULUS: Blessed be the Lord of Hosts!

LUMINOUS: Amen! His wisdom is infinite!

CUMULUS: There is no limit to his mercy!

LUMINOUS: Hallelujah! His love is everlasting!

CUMULUS: Give thanks to his glorious name!

LUMINOUS: In fact, the more hopeless, the better it is! It's a pretty amazing thing, this 'Gospel'!!

THIEF: Gospel? What's that?

LUMINOUS: Er, well, strictly speaking, it's really justification by faith through –

THIEF: Justin who?

LUMINOUS: (*Anxiously turning to* CUMULUS) We're going to have to do something about explaining this to people, you know.

CUMULUS: We may well have to rethink our theology.

THIEF: I can't see what zoology's got to do wiv it, mate. I was bein' executed for me crimes an' now I've landed up in Paradise. It's ff . . . flippin' marvellous!

LUMINOUS: Ff . . . Flippin' marvellous! Yes, that's quite a good way of putting it.

CUMULUS: Ff . . . Flippin' marvellous!

LUMINOUS: Hallelujah. Praise the Lord . . . (*All together*) It's ff . . . flippin' marvellous!!

In the Nick of Time

NARRATOR ONE; NARRATOR TWO; *characters in the mime*: A GROUSE; A GROUSE-SHOOTER; TWO CHRISTIANS; TWO ROMAN SOLDIERS; PETER, *the apostle*; FIGURE IN NIGHTMARE; ANGEL; SEVERAL MEMBERS OF PRAYER-GROUP, (*optional*); JAILER; SERVANT-GIRL

If the cast list of this sketch looks daunting, the characters in the mime could be played by three or four actors, using 'different hats' and making swift changes behind a central screen. Most of the movements of the mime must be left to the imagination and ingenuity of the director. The PRAYER-GROUP *is optional in that it can be suggested convincingly by the* NARRATORS' *dialogue. The sketch has also been performed very successfully with the various characters speaking their lines, where appropriate. The* NARRATORS *speak from either side of the stage.*

ONE: The most exciting . . .
TWO: Dynamic . . .
ONE: Radical . . .
TWO: Far-reaching . . .
ONE: And fundamental . . .
TWO: Changes in the history of the Church . . .
ONE: Have stemmed . . .
TWO: Almost entirely . . .
ONE: From grouse-hunting.
TWO: What's that?
ONE: Grouse-hunting.
TWO: What do you mean?
ONE: (*Insistently trying to reassure*) It's all right, everything's under control.
TWO: But, but . . .
ONE: This is a grouse. (*Enter* GROUSE)
TWO: (*Groans*)
ONE: 'I'm thoroughly fed up!'

TWO: BANG! (*Enter* GROUSE-SHOOTER)

ONE: 'One to me, Maurice.' (GROUSE *is dragged off*)

TWO: (*Coughs*) Has this anything to do with the Early Church?

ONE: Apparently.

TWO: Well, I have here, 'The Importance of House-meetings in the Early Church.'

ONE: Oh, *house*-meetings, not *grouse*-meetings?

TWO: No.

ONE: Ah, I see. I'm with you.

TWO: You've done it now.

ONE: No, wait, there's a perfect link. Listen.

TWO: Go on.

ONE: (*Beginning again*) Of all the sports in the Roman Empire . . .

TWO: The most popular was . . .

ONE: Hunt-the-Christian. (*Enter* CHRISTIAN)

TWO: (*Singing*) 'And can it be that I should – '

ONE: DUMPF! (CHRISTIAN *is knocked senseless by a* ROMAN SOLDIER *who has crept up behind her*)

TWO: 'One to me, Suetonius.' (*Body is dragged off*)

ONE: Life in the Early Church was never dull. (*Enter* SECOND CHRISTIAN)

TWO: It was challenging . . .

ONE: Inspiring . . .

TWO: Frequently brief . . .

ONE: And to the point. (CHRISTIAN *is summarily despatched with smart sword-thrust from* SECOND ROMAN SOLDIER)

TWO: 'One all, Marcellus.'

ONE: To be a Roman soldier in those days . . .

TWO: Was a demanding business.

ONE: It required skill . . .

TWO: Courage . . .

ONE: And great presence of mind. (*Exit* SOLDIER)

TWO: To be an apostle in those days . . . (*Enter* PETER)

ONE: Required faith . . .

TWO: Hope . . .

ONE: And considerable trust in God.

TWO: Such a man was Peter.

ONE: He confronted the Pharisees . . .

TWO: He confounded the lawyers . . .

ONE: He confused the authorities . . .

TWO: He converted the heathen . . .

ONE: And was clapped into jail. (NARRATORS *applaud*)

TWO: But throughout all this, as Head of the Church . . .

ONE: Peter was bald and hairless. (*Rechecking script*) I'm sorry, bold and fearless.

TWO: The Romans had bagged a big one.

ONE: Guarded by four squads of soldiers . . .

TWO: Handcuffed to his jailers . . .

ONE: Locked . . .

TWO: And double-locked . . .

ONE: Peter lay in the deepest dungeon . . .

TWO: Under sentence of death.

ONE: Now over to our sportsdesk in Rome.

TWO: Gladiators, 37.

ONE: Other gladiators, nil.

TWO: Lions, 52$^{1}/_{2}$.

ONE: Christians, $^{1}/_{2}$.

TWO: For Peter . . .

ONE: Things looked bleak.

TWO: Nonetheless, at the box-office, they looked good.

ONE: Peter's friends were justifiably alarmed.

TWO: That night they gathered for prayer.

ONE: They prayed fervently . . .

TWO: Earnestly . . .

ONE: With tears . . .

TWO: And sighs.

ONE: Imploring . . .

TWO: Beseeching . . .

ONE: Pleading . . .

TWO: Covering the situation with a mighty shield of intercession.

ONE: Pardon?

TWO: Sorry. So they prayed . . .

ONE: And prayed . . .

TWO: And prayed.

ONE: They just prayed, Lord, that God would surround Peter with his love, Father.

TWO: So he did.

ONE: They just prayed that if it be thy will, Lord . . .

TWO: Thou wouldst in some special way . . .

ONE: Perhaps . . .

TWO: Bless this situation, Father.

ONE: So he did.

TWO: They just prayed that in a very real sense,

ONE: O Lord . . .

TWO: Though humanly speaking it was hard to see how . . .

ONE: God would encourage Peter through his angels and ministers of light.

TWO: So he did. (FIGURE *enters prison where* PETER *is lying beside his* JAILER)

ONE: 'Pssst!'

TWO: (*As* PETER) 'Whassat!?'

ONE: 'It's me going "pssst".'

TWO: 'Who are you?'

ONE: 'The Pssst-man. Bye.' (*Exit* FIGURE)

TWO: Peter had many similar nightmares.

ONE: So when God sent an angel. (*Enter* ANGEL)

TWO: He thought he was dreaming.

ONE: But his chains fell off and woke him up.

TWO: 'Good Heavens!' said Peter.

ONE: 'Precisely,' said the angel.

TWO: 'But how?' said Peter.

ONE: 'Airmail,' said the angel.

TWO: 'Sorry to be so bright and early.

ONE: Hang on, I'll turn myself off.'

TWO: (*Click.* ANGEL *reduces glare from halo*)

ONE: 'Thanks.'

TWO: 'Now follow me,' said the angel.

ONE: 'It is *Peter*, isn't it?'

TWO: 'Yes.'

ONE: 'Cell forty-one?'

TWO: 'Yes.'

ONE: 'Right, follow me.'

TWO: Past the guards . . .

ONE: Through the doors . . .

TWO: Down the steps . . .

ONE: Across the courtyard . . .

TWO: Through the iron gates . . .

ONE: And into the streets of the city.

TWO: 'Sign here,' said the angel.

ONE: 'What for?'

TWO: 'Recorded delivery.'

ONE: 'Stand by for take-off.'

TWO: 'Righto, Algie.'

ONE: 'Over and out.'

TWO: (*Noise of sudden airborne departure. Exit* ANGEL)

ONE: Peter came to himself.

TWO: 'Hullo. Is that Peter?'

ONE: 'Yes.'

TWO: 'Follow me.'

ONE: (*To other* NARRATOR) Shut up.

TWO: Sorry.

ONE: Soon he arrived outside the house where his friends were praying.

TWO: He knocked loudly.

ONE: (*Knocking*)

TWO: 'O Lord, we do just continue to pray, Father . . .

ONE: That you will come to our brother Peter in his cell . . .

TWO: Encouraging him . . .

ONE: Supporting him . . .

TWO: Assuring him that he has not been forgotten.

ONE: (*Knocking*)

TWO: And let us not be distracted, Lord.

ONE: (*Knocking*)

TWO: Lord, as you look down on Peter now . . .

ONE: We pray, Father, that you will hear his cry.'

TWO: 'Open up!'

ONE: 'And Lord, whoever that is . . .

TWO: Calm him . . .

ONE: And give him your peace.'

TWO: 'LET ME IN!'

ONE: And so, as Peter stood knocking at the door . . .

TWO: A servant-girl had the sense to answer it.
ONE: 'Who is it?'
TWO: (*As if through letterbox*) 'Peter.'
ONE: She recognised his voice.
TWO: Her heart leapt into her mouth.
ONE: (*Gulp*)
TWO: Her legs turned to jelly.
ONE: (*Fllobbalobalob*)
TWO: She ran back to the prayer meeting.
ONE: 'It's Peter! It's Peter!'
TWO: 'O Lord, we do ask – what's that?'
ONE: 'It's Peter!'
TWO: 'Yes, dear, we're praying for him.'
ONE: 'Shall I let him in?'
TWO: 'Not now, dear, we're praying for Peter.'
ONE: 'He's standing outside.'
TWO: 'Ask him for two pints and we'll pay him on Thursday.'
ONE: (*Knocking*)
TWO: 'OPEN UP!!'
ONE: 'I told you, it's Peter!'
TWO: 'You're mad.'
ONE: (*Knocking*)
TWO: 'IT'S ME, PETER!'
ONE: 'You know what?'
TWO: 'What?'
ONE: 'That sounds like Peter outside.'
TWO: 'The very thing we were praying for, Hallelujah.'
ONE: 'Hallelujah.'
TWO: 'Praise the Lord!'
ONE: 'WILL YOU LET ME IN!'
TWO: 'Oh, yes.' So they did.
ONE: Now when you turn to prayer,
TWO: Remember that he's there.
ONE: His angels know the score,
TWO: They've been down here before.

Postal Orders

ZOE, *a recent convert to Christianity and member of the church in Corinth; former cult prostitute in the local temple of Aphrodite*; THE APOSTLE PAUL, *in Ephesus, writing the first letter to the Corinthian church*

Major pastoral problems abounded in the Corinthian church. One does not have to read very deeply between the lines of Paul's lengthy letters to grasp the extent to which the church was becoming infected with the general immorality of the sea port in which it had been established. At the same time, dealing with these problems brings out of Paul some of the most moving and evocative writing in the New Testament. This sketch is a reminder that Paul wrote practical letters to groups of ordinary people for whom he cared very much. It attempts to reveal a little of the dramatic context behind the business of pastoring by post.

An obvious way to stage this sketch would be to use two pools of light to isolate the two actors, one in Corinth and one in Ephesus. At the very least, the writing of the letter and the telephone conversation should be set on either side of the performing space. At the start, PAUL *is seated at his desk;* ZOE's *phone rings. She enters to answer it.*

ZOE: (*Answering*) Phoebe! Hi! How was the holiday? (*Pause*) Of course we have. Corinth has been lost without you, m'dear. Well, the church has, certainly. (*Pause while Phoebe speaks*) Oooh, the usual tensions and holy infighting, I would say. Who's in charge, who's sleeping with whom, hats on or off to pray, you know the stuff . . . (*Her voice fades, although she continues the conversation silently*)

PAUL: (*Reading back to himself his opening sentences*) From Paul, chosen by God to be an apostle of Christ Jesus. To

the Christians in Corinth, called to be a holy people united
with God's Son, Jesus Christ, our Lord. (*He continues to
type rapidly as he speaks*) I thank God for you every day.
I long to visit you but unfortunately I can't get away from
Ephesus for the time being. The weather hasn't exactly
been brilliant . . . better not put that in. (*He deletes it*)
However, I want to reply to the very important questions
put to me by your elders, Stephanas, Fortunatus and
Achaicus, who are, as you know, on a pastoral visit here
at the moment . . . (*His voice fades as he continues to type
the letter*)

ZOE: Who did you say? Started his diet yet? Gaius?
Chance'd be a fine thing! Last week he was stuffing
his face with marinated squid and vine leaves in church.
Yes! During the communion service! So embarrassing.
Especially with poor old Tychicus standing there with all
his starving kids. The whole thing was way out of control.
Demetrius got completely plastered, dropped his napkin in
the cup and spilt the wine all down his trousers. By the
end of the service he was dancing round the room with a
herb sausage, singing, 'We shall rise, on that resurrection
morning we shall rise.' I had to leave . . . (*Fade*)

PAUL: (*Tapping away forcefully*) Anyone who eats the bread
and drinks the cup of Christ in an unworthy manner is
guilty of profaning the body and blood of the Lord.
Communion is about proclaiming Christ's death until he
comes again. Not an excuse for a drunken picnic!!! (*To
himself as he types them*) Triple exclamation marks. That
is why many of you are weak and ill . . . (*Fade*)

ZOE: The elders weren't there, of course. You know,
Stephanas, Fortunatus and Achaicus. No, off seeing that
Paul in sunny Ephesus. 'Church Leaders' Conference' or
something. Apparently we might all be getting a letter
from Paul. I know. I know. He is a bit. Many people
seem to prefer that other lad who baptised me at Easter,
what-do-they-call-him, Apollos. Lydia says she could listen
to his voice for hours. Actually, I think Lydia's more
impressed with his legs. She's going from bad to worse
at the moment . . . (*Fade*)

PAUL: (*Stirring a mug of coffee*) What's this I hear about quarrelling among you? Factions! Even law-suits! (*Typing angrily*) 'I belong to Paul', 'I belong to Apollos'. Who *are* Paul and Apollos, for goodness sake? Were you baptised into *Paul*? . . . (*Fade*)

ZOE: He's living with her, Phoebe! Well, Lydia's his father's wife, isn't she?! . . . (*Fade*)

PAUL: Apollos and I are just the people who helped you to believe. Nothing! God does all the work. But I'm not trying to shame you. I love you. You're my children in Christ (*To himself*) and I wish you'd grow up . . . (*Fade*)

ZOE: Talk about new freedom in Jesus. Mmmn? (*Pause*) Well, I wouldn't have thought it was *that* common to shack up with your father's wife, even in this city of sin. Unbelievers have some standards. He needs a straight talking to . . . (*Fade*)

PAUL: He must be expelled from the church. Bad yeast ruins the whole loaf. Christians ought not . . . No. (*Retyping*) *Cannot* condone the sins that Christ died for. (*Loading a new page and referring to a list*) All these questions. (*Typing fast*) Taking one another to court is a *disaster* for the church . . . (*Fade*)

ZOE: But Phoebe, I thought I was leaving all that pagan filth behind me when I joined the church. I don't know where I am. Just because Jason and his crowd can eat in the temples doesn't mean that I can. According to them, 'idols don't really exist'. Well, I spent two years on my back for Aphrodite and that felt real enough . . . (*Fade*)

PAUL: (*Composing his thoughts before writing*) Love is the best way to build up the church. Real love. Patient, kind, unselfish love. Love that always protects, always trusts, never fails. (*Typing*) One day, faith, hope and love will be the only things left to us. But the most important of these is love. So, let everything you do be done in love . . . (*Fade*)

ZOE: I just long for someone to start telling me the truth, giving me something to live for that's simple and different. Do you know what I mean? . . .

PAUL: The grace of the Lord Jesus be with you. (*He*

*removes the page and signs it. He puts the letter into an
envelope and seals it*) I wonder if I've got any stamps?
(PAUL *goes off in search of stamps.* ZOE *replaces the
telephone*)

A Little Further Advice

(*For those unhappy with I Corinthians 13 as it stands*)

This a short reading from Not-Paul's-first-letter-to-the-Corinthians. For the purposes of satirising an attitude apparently much admired in Britain in the late twentieth century, this piece deliberately twists some of the most well-known and important words in the whole Bible. (See the introduction to 'A Little Advice from the Mount' on page 60)

If I speak with the tongues of men and of angels, but have not aggression, I am a namby-pamby and a windy-wet-legs. And if I have political powers and understand all problems, both social and economic, and if I enter all disputes, but have not aggression, I am nothing. If I cling on to all my possessions and protect myself at all costs, without aggression, I am done for. Aggression is fruitless and harsh. Aggression is not humble or caring but arrogant and rude. Aggression always insists on its own way, avoiding discussion or compromise. It is proud and strong; it lashes out at once when its interests are threatened and rejoices at another's defeat. Aggression hurts all things, tramples all things, breaks all things, destroys all things. Aggression always ends in tears. So fear, greed and aggression abide, these three; but the greatest of these is self.

One Faith, One Lord

THREE CHRISTIANS

To the uninitiated observer the Christian Church must seem very puzzling. Over the centuries, Christians have often stressed their differences, yet they all claim to be followers of Christ. What is the outsider to think? Will he really have the patience to discover the distinctions between a Methodist and a Baptist, a Free Churchman and a Plymouth Brother, a charismatic Anglican and a renewed Presbyterian, 'high' and Roman Catholic? To him, the Church must look very similar to the Football League: everybody is basically following the same game, while fanatically supporting different players, in different colours, some teams with a reputation for fancy footwork and attacking flair, others for simply thumping the ball into the goalmouth. A cursory glance shows the Church to be more divided than united. The Bible teaches that love never insists on its own way, so perhaps a sketch such as this, which makes fun of some of these differences, can put them in perspective and show how cosmetic they really are. Taste in worship is one thing, faith in our 'one Lord and Saviour, Jesus Christ' is quite another and much more important.

THREE CHRISTIANS (*they could be men or women or, preferably, a mixture) file on to the stage, solemnly humming the tune to the hymn, 'Thy hand, O God, has guided Thy flock from age to age.' They take up positions at the front. Their attitudes, clothes and mode of address to the audience tell us that they are different, though these distinctions are subtle, not cartooned. The third Christian is the most casual and has a warm, friendly, almost off-hand way of delivering the lines.*

ONE: My church is a high church.

TWO: My church is a low church.

THREE: (*Momentarily stuck for something apt*) My church is above sea-level. (*He shrugs*)

ONE: Besides the altar, we have chalices, chasubles, candles, acolytes and wafers.

TWO: Besides the Lord's Table, we have psalters, robes, lecterns, notice-boards and real bread.

THREE: Beside the piano, we have a box for the hymnbooks.

ONE: I find great meaning in ritual and ceremony.

TWO: I find great meaning in extempore prayer and exposition.

THREE: I don't know what any of them mean!

ONE: I read the Authorised King James Version. It has real beauty.

TWO: I read the Revised Standard Version. It has real authority.

THREE: I read the Good News Version. It's got real pictures.

ONE: We are rediscovering the charismatic essence of the liturgy of the Church.

TWO: We are rediscovering the principles of charismatic renewal in the life of the congregation.

THREE: I'm not sure, but I think our washing machine's charismatic.

ONE: We celebrate the Eucharist.

TWO: We share the Lord's Supper.

THREE: We never know what to call it either.

ONE: We always finish prayer with a suitable collect.

TWO: We always finish prayer by saying the grace.

THREE: We always finish prayer in time to watch the snooker (*Or name of current TV programme*)

ONE: Next Sunday is Quinquagesima.

TWO: Next Sunday is the beginning of our Lent Course.

THREE: (*Obviously impressed with the others but cannot compete*)
Er, next Sunday's the fourteenth, isn't it?

ONE: I find the lectionary a great source of meditation.

TWO: I find the sermons a great source of spiritual encouragement.

THREE: I find the pews a great source of backache.

ONE: Our worship is tastefully enhanced by a combination of Stanford, Tallis, Byrd and Gibbons.

TWO: Our worship is doctrinally balanced by a combination of Wesley, Watts and the Redemption Hymnal.

THREE: Our worship is definitely *ruined* by a combination of a tone-deaf worship leader and choruses with eighty-three repeats of the last verse.

ONE: We have coffee in the narthex after matins.

TWO: We have bring-and-share lunches in the hall after service.

THREE: (*With deep loathing*) We have tea in green cups after *everything*!

ONE: The discipline of the Daily Office frees my spirit to meditate on higher things.

TWO: The length of the prayers allows me time for personal devotion.

THREE: Yeah, my mind tends to wander a bit, too.

ONE: But Christ is the Head of our Church.

TWO: Christ is the Cornerstone of our faith.

THREE: Christ is the Rock on which we build.
(*They look at each other for a moment, encouraged yet puzzled by their unexpected agreement*)

ONE: (*Returning to the audience*) But I think *our* way of doing things is most *reverent*.

TWO: I think *our* way of doing things is truly *biblical*.

THREE: I'm sure there's a lot of prejudice in *our* church as well.

(*As each says the final line they turn away slightly. Freeze.*)

Note. We are indebted to Phil Potter for suggesting the theme of this sketch.

Spreading the Word Around a Bit

GEOFF; ANDREW; MICHAEL, *members of the same church fellowship*

The Bible has some stern things to say about the subject of gossip. In the letter to the church at Rome, Paul numbers gossips among those who 'did not see fit to acknowledge God'; they 'reveal secrets' and 'say what they should not'. Gossip might well be seen as one of the 'little foxes' that destroy the vineyard of the church. It is therefore a satiric target that is well worth hitting hard, particularly by avoiding the stereotyped attitude that this is a female problem – men are equally guilty. Many of the things said in this sketch might seem innocuous enough, but the destructive power of gossip is so often covered by a well-meaning veneer, achieving its end by hints, half-truths and subtleties of motive and expression. There is, however, nothing subtle about the intentional violence of the final sequence. It is inspired by St Paul's warning to the Galatian church (chapter 5, verse 15): 'If you bite and devour one another, take heed that you are not consumed by one another.'

GEOFF, ANDREW and MICHAEL enter and stand facing away from the audience towards the back of the stage. They remain in these positions except when they come forward to speak. GEOFF and ANDREW turn to the audience. They are in mid-conversation.

GEOFF: Look, you won't say anything, Andrew, will you? Because Gill would be really upset.

ANDREW: Of course.

GEOFF: If people knew . . .

ANDREW: Well, they mustn't.

GEOFF: I just wanted you to know, that's all.

ANDREW: Right.

GEOFF: I wish I knew what to do.

ANDREW: It's extremely hard to know. There seem to be so many problems around these days. Michael had a very serious disagreement with Brian the other day. They were at each other's throats.

GEOFF: Michael!

ANDREW: Oh yes.

GEOFF: Good grief, I'd never have guessed it of him.

ANDREW: I'd never have guessed it of him either – I was told. Still, I think he's sorted it all out now. Just.

GEOFF: How do you mean 'just'?

ANDREW: Well, Michael's so . . .

GEOFF: Yes, I know what you mean.

ANDREW: I wouldn't want to give you the wrong impression, Geoff. Michael's a really nice guy, but you just don't know where you are with him.

GEOFF: It's strange you should say that, because I've been a little uneasy about Michael sometimes. I remember him at that house-party.

ANDREW: That's a very good example of what I'm talking about. (*Their conversation fades off.* MICHAEL *steps forward to join* ANDREW)

MICHAEL: I hear Geoff won't be with us on Tuesday, Andrew.

ANDREW: No, I don't think he will, Michael.

MICHAEL: Is he all right?

ANDREW: I think it's fair to say he's been under attack recently.

MICHAEL: I gather it's been a difficult year.

ANDREW: On and off. He shared quite a lot with me last night, actually.

MICHAEL: Did he?

ANDREW: Yes. It's a difficult thing to face on one's own. I don't know, but I think he was encouraged by what I said.

MICHAEL: It's been pretty grim, so Doreen tells me.

ANDREW: Oh, you know a bit about the situation, then?

MICHAEL: Only what I've gleaned here and there. The odd comment.

ANDREW: In that case you've probably gathered –

MICHAEL: Sonia?

ANDREW: Well, she's involved. A lot of it does surround her. Look, Michael, this is obviously only for your ears and prayers, but the other night things blew up again.

MICHAEL: Really? (*They turn away, still talking, as* GEOFF *steps forward to join* MICHAEL)

GEOFF: It's incredible!

MICHAEL: I don't know how he justifies it.

GEOFF: Three hundred quid!

MICHAEL: Easily.

GEOFF: Just for the skis.

MICHAEL: On top of hotels, food, ski passes, rail fares . . .

GEOFF: No, they both flew. And the children.

MICHAEL: Right, well, we're obviously talking about eight or nine hundred quid.

GEOFF: Each.

MICHAEL: Where on earth does Andrew get all his money from?

GEOFF: I dunno. They're always talking about not having enough.

MICHAEL: No wonder, is it?

GEOFF: I think it's thoroughly irresponsible.

MICHAEL: (*Pause*) Why *did* they ask him to be a lay preacher?

GEOFF: Wouldn't have been my choice.

MICHAEL: Still, he's got his good side.

GEOFF: But he's hardly ever at home with his family, you know. (*At this point,* ANDREW *steps forward on the other side of* MICHAEL, *who freezes. As each pair speak, they punctuate the ends of their remarks by miming the tearing off and eating of strips of flesh from the third. In each case the 'victim' stands motionless between his assailants. While maintaining a conversational tone, the accompanying actions should be savage*)

GEOFF: You just don't know where you are with someone like Michael.

ANDREW: I wouldn't want to give you the wrong impression.

MICHAEL: I gather it's been a difficult year for Geoff.
ANDREW: He's been really under attack recently.

MICHAEL: He wouldn't have been my choice.
GEOFF: I think he's thoroughly irresponsible.

GEOFF: I'm a bit concerned about Michael's attitude.
ANDREW: He's just out to please himself.

MICHAEL: Geoff's faith used to be so strong.
ANDREW: Things seem to be going from bad to worse.

MICHAEL: Andrew was the one I always turned to for advice.
GEOFF: Funny the way things have changed.

Violence in the Home

TV ANNOUNCER; MOTHER; FATHER; DAUGHTER; SON; VOICE

The teaching of Jesus was often aimed at the 'law-abiding' citizen who felt self-righteous. The sketch typifies this familiar attitude of detachment from the evil in the world, a habit of mind frequently worsened by television viewing. In addition to its relevance, an actor sitting behind a hollowed-out television set and reading the news is a useful eye-catcher for street audiences.

The stage setting is an ordinary living-room. For open air performance, no more is needed than a few surfaces to sit on, chairs if available, and the television set with the ANNOUNCER *seated behind it. The* SON *lounges across two chairs, the* DAUGHTER *sits disconsolately, the* MOTHER *goes over to switch on the news.*

ANNOUNCER: Good evening. Tragedy hits a home in North London. A man was arrested today after attacking his wife and two children with a sledge hammer. All three have since died. The children, Richard aged nine, and Elizabeth aged eight, had recently been sent to a new school but had come home for the holidays. The man, John Harris, thirty-one, said earlier today, 'I didn't mean to kill them. I got annoyed. I lost control.' He pleaded not guilty to charges of violence with intent to kill. More news about the threatened strike in the National Health Service . . .

(MOTHER *switches off television*)

MOTHER: I think it's terrible that anybody should do that. There's nothing but violence on the news. How could anybody do that? I don't see how a man could just go and kill his wife and children.

(*Enter* HUSBAND)

Why are you late? You said you'd be here at four o'clock.

You never come when you say. I wanted us to go shopping together this afternoon. You never think of others, do you? You're so selfish!

(*As she says this, she points at him to emphasise her words. The* HUSBAND *dies as if he were shot by a gun*)

(*In some circumstances, the damaging nature of swearwords can be indicated by adding one to 'selfish' – we have generally done this on the streets and in clubs, but not in church, where attitudes of anger rather than specific bad language tend to be the problem. It can be right to demonstrate the implications of swearing in anger, but it is senseless to cause offence by doing this if the problem is not a relevant one*)

VOICE: (*During this the action freezes*) You want things but you cannot have them so you quarrel and fight. You want things and you cannot get them so you are ready to kill.

MOTHER: (*As her* DAUGHTER *gets up to go*) You're not going out looking like that, are you? That dress hangs on you like a sack. Why can't you be like Claire next door? She's got real taste.

(*The* DAUGHTER *dies. Freeze*)

VOICE: The tongue is like a fire. It is a world of wrong spreading evil through our whole being. No man has ever been able to control it.

(*The* MOTHER, *oblivious to the effect of her words, turns to her* SON)

MOTHER: Out! Go on, get out! After all I've done for you, you sit on your backside lazing around. You make me sick!

(*The* SON *falls off the chair and dies. Freeze*)

VOICE: You have been told 'do not murder'. But I say to you, anyone who is angry with his brother has already committed murder.

(*The* MOTHER *goes over and switches on the television*)

ANNOUNCER: Good evening. Here is the late news. Tragedy hits a home in North London. A man was arrested today after attacking his wife and two children with a sledge hammer. All three have since died. The children, Richard aged nine, and Elizabeth aged eight, had recently been sent to a new school but had come home for the holidays. The man, John Harris, thirty-one, said earlier today, 'I didn't mean to kill them. I got annoyed. I lost control.' He pleaded not guilty to charges of violence with intent to kill. (*The* MOTHER *switches off the television*)

MOTHER: (*To the audience*) How can anybody do a thing like that?

The Examination

FOUR DEVILS: DR CUNNINGHAM, *young female*; PROFESSOR TWIST, *suave, middle-aged*; DR GLOAT, *pinched, middle-aged woman*; DR leFACTS, *eccentric and octogenarian*; J.S. NICHOLL, *a hesitant Christian*

Temptation is not an easy subject to deal with in a way that is educational as well as entertaining. In The Screwtape Letters, *C.S. Lewis has memorably satirised the works of the devil, with many flashes of wit and humour, albeit of a somewhat chilling nature. At the beginning of the book, he quotes Martin Luther: 'The best way to drive out the devil, if he will not yield to texts of Scripture, is to jeer and flout him, for he cannot bear scorn.' In a similar way, this sketch uses humour to illuminate a very serious subject: temptation leads to sin, which leads to death, and it is this biblical equation on which the sketch finally turns. Jesus refuted the temptations in the wilderness by quoting the written Word of God, and thorough knowledge of the Bible is still a primary weapon against the devil today.*

The scene will be particularly familiar to students since it is set in a university 'viva voce', or oral examination. Four chairs are placed on three sides of a large table, on which there is a telephone. Another chair is set facing the table at an angle, but isolated from it. Enter PROFESSOR TWIST, DR GLOAT *and* DR leFACTS *in academic dress, carrying sheaves of paper. They sit around the table, impatiently waiting for* DR CUNNINGHAM *to fill the fourth chair. After a pause, she enters.*

CUNNINGHAM: No apologies for being late, Professor. (*Sits*)

TWIST: Bad, bad. Well, I suppose we'd better get a move on. The world may be drawing to a close and we've got all these people to tempt before the Last Judgement. Now, who've we got next?

GLOAT: Excuse me, Professor, but I do find Earth rather chilly. Can we do anything about it?

TWIST: Try a bit of hell*fire*, I suppose. (*General chuckles*) Perhaps Dr leFacts would care to lend you his gown, though I realise it's hardly within his nature to do so?

leFACTS: (*Chuckling*) Not likely.

TWIST: Bad. Shall we proceed? Our next candidate appears to be J. S. Nicholl. I trust you have his papers in front of you.

CUNNINGHAM: Shall I call him in, Professor?

TWIST: Why not? He should be suitably nervous by now.

GLOAT: Before you do, Inferna, am I not right in thinking that this person is a Christian? (*General groans*) So it, er, might be a little trickier than the last one.

TWIST: Hell's bells. (*Phone rings*) Hullo? (*Covering phone*) Talk of the devil. (*Back to phone*) Yes, sir, of course, sir. We were just about to begin the temptation when you rang. Oh, really? That's very bad of you. Aha, mmm. Well, thank you for being so impatient with us. (*Makes face at phone as he hangs up. It burns his hand*)

CUNNINGHAM: I see the hot-line's still functional. Shall I get him now?

TWIST: Please. (CUNNINGHAM *exits and returns with* NICHOLL)
Ah, Nicholl.

NICHOLL: (*Correcting him*) J. Nicholl actually, sir. ('*We've got a right one here*' looks from examiners)

TWIST: Just sit down, Mr Nicholl. Now, we've read your papers on Biblical Knowledge with considerable disinterest and we would like to ask you a few questions arising out of your answers, if you see what I mean? Fire away, then, chaps.

leFACTS: Do the words 'Viva Voce' mean anything to you, Mr Nicholl?

NICHOLL: No, I'm afraid not.

leFACTS: No, I've never understood them myself. Thank you, Professor.

GLOAT: Mr Nicholl, what precise evidence do you find in the Bible to support your statement here that, I quote, 'God loves you'?

NICHOLL: Well, er, yes, there's a famous verse, erm . . . somewhere in Matthew, I think . . .

GLOAT: 'Somewhere in Matthew'. How deliciously vague. Can you quote it, Mr Nicholl?

NICHOLL: No. I'm sorry.

GLOAT: Oh, please. Don't start being *sorry* for anything here. (*Much chuckling among examiners*)

leFACTS: (*Highly amused*) 'Sorry', ahaha!

TWIST: (*Trying to recover a sense of seriousness*) Mr Nicholl, can you explain why your answer on the miracles of Jesus made no reference to the miracle of the bricks being turned into water?

NICHOLL: I don't recall ever reading that one, sir.

TWIST: Come, come, Mr Nicholl, surely you have read the gospel according to Norman?

NICHOLL: I don't think so, sir.

TWIST: It comes just after Luke.

CUNNINGHAM: You'll find it a lot less helpful than some of the others.

TWIST: Did you have a question, Dr Cunningham?

CUNNINGHAM: Yes. (*Posing provocatively on edge of table. Speaking huskily*) Mr Nicholl, how do you understand the concept of temptation?

GLOAT: I doubt that he will fall for anything as obvious as that, Inferna.

CUNNINGHAM: There's no point in making things too subtle, sweetie, this one's hardly been known to fail. (*Resuming husky voice*) Mr Nicholl?

NICHOLL: (*Sweating*) Well, erm, temptation is an external pressure on the individual conscience, which – well, internal, too, I suppose – a pressure to deviate . . .

CUNNINGHAM: Yes?

NICHOLL: To deviate from what one believes to be fundamentally true; truth being something which is defined and received from God and contained in his Word.

CUNNINGHAM: And who told you all that, Mr Nicholl?

NICHOLL: God did.

CUNNINGHAM: God *speaks* to you? How?

NICHOLL: Through his Word.

CUNNINGHAM: But who told you *that*, Mr Nicholl?

NICHOLL: God did.

CUNNINGHAM: I see. Thank you, Professor.

leFACTS: (*Clearing throat*) Aren't we getting our wires crossed a little here, Mr Nicholl? I must say I'm very surprised to hear you speak of the Bible as, shall we say, the Fountain-head of Truth. Perhaps in your studies, wide though your reading may have been, you have overlooked my colleague Professor Twist's own work on biblical inconsistency. Do you not find any evidence for this in, say, the book of Proverbs?

NICHOLL: I can't say that I've ever considered it.

leFACTS: Well, er, 'Too many cooks spoil the broth', yet 'Many hands make light work'. I mean, what do you make of it?

NICHOLL: Are those both *in* Proverbs, sir?

leFACTS: You tell me, Mr Nicholl, after all, it is not I who am being examined, is it?

NICHOLL: I'm afraid I don't know the answer, sir.

TWIST: You must avoid being too honest in your replies, Mr Nicholl. Now, I should like to move on to another question. Would you say that material prosperity has ever influenced your academic career?

NICHOLL: (*Sharply*) No.

TWIST: It's all right, it's all right. Just tempting.

GLOAT: Your overall haziness on the book of Proverbs prompts me to ask another question. Your written answers make almost exclusive reference to material drawn from the New Testament, in particular the epistles. Do you only read the short ones, Mr Nicholl?

NICHOLL: I have read the Old Testament.

GLOAT: Summarise for me the message of the book of Deuteronomy.

NICHOLL: That's near the beginning, isn't it? Well, it's . . . um . . .

GLOAT: You're doing very well, Mr Nicholl.

NICHOLL: It's about Moses and the Israelites and sacrificing.

TWIST: Have you ever thought of publishing your research, Mr Nicholl? I mean, I think you can afford to take considerable pride in your work. At least, you'll certainly be able to afford it once you've published. (*Shares private joke*) Ahem. Fine. Why didn't you answer the question on the irrelevance of prayer?

NICHOLL: I had already answered three questions and I happen to find it very relevant.

TWIST: The question?

NICHOLL: No, prayer.

TWIST: But you haven't answered my question, Mr Nicholl.

NICHOLL: I have answered your question.

TWIST: Am I making you angry?

NICHOLL: Yes.

TWIST: Good.

CUNNINGHAM: Mr Nicholl, would you mind completing the quotation, 'the wages of sin are . . .'?

NICHOLL: Um . . . er . . .

CUNNINGHAM: Bad?

leFACTS: Low, compared with the national average? (*General chuckling*)

NICHOLL: That's not right. It's 'the wages of sin *is* . . .', you've misquoted it.

CUNNINGHAM: That's what we're here for.

NICHOLL: 'The wages of sin is death.' (*All four examiners sit up sharply, drawing in breath and glaring at* NICHOLL. *There is an icy atmosphere*)

leFACTS: No need to overstate it, Mr Nicholl.

TWIST: That sort of knowledge won't get you very far, will it?

GLOAT: That will probably be all for now, Professor.

CUNNINGHAM: What a pity we had to end on such an awkward note.

TWIST: Mr Nicholl, don't hesitate to be in touch if we can be of any further hindrance to you. (*Exit* NICHOLL. *Lights fade out on the* DEVILS *bickering and muttering together over the table*)

The Weather Forecast

KLAUDIA SPELTZ, *a TV 'weather caster'*

This sketch hardly requires an introduction. A glance at any weather forecast will give a clear idea of the setting (large maps with appropriate symbols will add a great deal to the effect) and a study of the speech will show that it requires regular updating in certain places. Whoever is introducing the sketch can take on the role of the TV continuity man or woman, with 'And now a look at the world weather situation with Klaudia Speltz.'

KLAUDIA: Well, little change really. North-east Africa will continue to suffer a major famine. This will move in from the south-west and not clear up after lunch. For those of you who've booked expensive holidays in Europe, don't worry, it won't affect Chamonix, Paris or Bournemouth. Refugees will continue to move steadily from Ethiopia to Sudan, fleeing from one place without food to another. As you can imagine, from satellite information taken at midday, this all happens well to the south of the Sussex–Kent border.

The longer-range forecast, then. There will be scattered intervals of political and social awareness during the rest of the century, but these will die out fairly soon after the next G7 summit meeting, giving way to a period of heated discussion within major broadcasting networks about internal market forces and the terrible price of kitchen extensions these days. This will encourage a change in the prevailing wind of public concern, and before long a large number of social and political factors will cloud over the issue of massive Western responsibility for the Third World.

The outlook, then, for the year. Around the end of December, an alcoholic haze will descend, creating a thick blanket of fog in people's minds, and some rather blotchy faces. This will give way to thundery spells in the lavatory but it's fair to say that most heads will clear during the first week of January. Over this period, a few hundred thousand children will have died of starvation, but, generally speaking, this fact will be kept well away from our television screens.

The summary, then: no rain over much of Africa, but extremely heavy showers over Wimbledon, the Henley Regatta and many golf courses, I'm afraid. Otherwise a generally smug feeling settling over most of the northern hemisphere, and a nice warm front in the Bundesbank. So an ideal climate then for all those with private health care but a good deal of frost forming in the hearts of our political leaders.

That's all from me, goodnight.

The Evangelical Mission to the Poor and Needy

LADY, *Mrs Fervent, media-conscious Chair of a national organisation*; ONE, *personal assistant to Mrs Fervent*; TWO, *secretary*

This sketch (originally published as the final section of 'The Good Old Ways' in Red Letter Days*) is a dramatic commentary on the teaching of the epistle of James that deals with the hollowness which arises when 'faith' is not accompanied by 'works', and vice versa. 'Suppose,' says James, 'a brother or sister is without clothes or daily food. If one of you says to him "Go, I wish you well. Keep warm and well fed," but does nothing about his physical needs, what good is it? So faith by itself, if it is not accompanied by action, is dead.' James does not mince his words. Others have expressed the same truth in terms of a pair of scissors: unless the two blades of faith and action work together, the gospel has no cutting edge. In Matthew chapter twenty-five, Jesus reminds the righteous, who claim never to have failed Jesus in practical service, that as often as they neglected the poor, the weak and the prisoner, they were neglecting him. The consequences of this neglect are frightening and yet how easy it is for us to become blinded by a welter of religious activity and so miss the many, small, God-given opportunities day by day to share the love of Christ with others.*

A phone rings on a desk to one side of the stage. The LADY *answers it.*

LADY: Ah, good morning. This is the Evangelical Mission to the Poor and Needy, what can I do for you . . .? Right, we'll do everything we can to help you . . . pray for you, send you money, organise a campaign for you . . . speak at your meeting, certainly. Goodbye and God bless you.

ONE: Excuse me, Mrs Fervent, your daughter's on the other line. She needs to speak to you urgently.

LADY: Can you tell her to call me back? I can't speak to her just now.

ONE: She says she's very depressed and needs to spend some time with you.

LADY: Tell her I'll . . . I'll speak to her this evening. (*The phone rings*) Hello, Evangelical Mission to the Poor and Needy . . . Ah, Mr Zealous, good morning . . . I'll certainly organise that rally for you . . . we'd like to give you every support.

TWO: Excuse me, Mrs Fervent, it's your next-door neighbour, she's popped in to ask whether you'd like to come round for a sherry.

LADY: That's rather awkward. I don't drink and – oh, my goodness, I'm supposed to be at the Missionary Prayer Fellowship – can you put her off?

TWO: She looks a little down . . . spoke of her husband.

LADY: Oh yes, he left her apparently. Tell her I'd love to come over sometime in the near future. (*Back to the phone*) So sorry about that interruption, Mr Zealous . . . could you put me on to Mrs Enthusiasm, I'd be so grateful, bless you. Hello, Mrs Enthusiasm, this is the Evangelical Mission to the Poor and Needy . . . yes, yes . . . bless you . . . well, I really have appreciated all your support over the years, and I must thank you for your generous gifts . . . Certainly, I'd be more than happy to speak at the Women's Group . . . diary's a bit full . . . what about the fifteenth of August? Super, bless you, goodbye.

ONE: There's a man at the door who smells of drink . . . says he lives in the basement flat over the road . . .

LADY: Just a minute. (*Writing in her diary*) Fifteenth of August, Women's Group, 3.30 . . . hymns and readings to be chosen by the seventh of August. Now look, can you give this man some money and tell him it's difficult to find any jobs for him at the moment. (*Phone rings*) Hello, Evangelical Mission to the Poor and Needy . . . yes . . . yes . . . BBC Radio 4! *Thought for the Day*? How soon? Fine, I'd love to . . . bless you, I'll be in touch.

TWO: Another visitor has just called, Mrs Fervent, but he
went away.

LADY: Thank goodness for that. This is getting ridiculous!

TWO: He left this card. (*Hands it to her*)

LADY: (*Reading*) Jesus called but found you unavailable.
(*She is horror-stricken. There is a short silence. The* TWO
OFFICE WORKERS *echo the line as the lights fade*)

TWO: Unavailable . . .

ONE: Jesus called . . .

TWO: But found you unavailable . . .

ONE: Unavailable . . .

Here Beginneth the Second Lesson
by Nigel Forde

MR FLETCHER, *a teacher of Ancient History, middle-aged, slightly stuffy, thinks he is one of the lads;* CULSHAW, *a schoolboy. Lazy but very bright, the bane of every teacher's existence;* SAMANTHA, *will one day be a hairdresser;* DOREEN, *quite bright but a bit of a plodder; admires Culshaw immensely;* BRISTER, *can just about spell 'and'; sometimes sits the right way up but seldom moves.*

The main thing to beware of in this sketch is lack of discipline among those playing the schoolchildren. Theoretically, any number of extra actors can be used to fill out the class, but the danger of upstaging the action is thereby increased. In many ways it takes more experience to play a bit-part than a main character. It is a fairly static sketch – the only actor who can move is he who plays the teacher – and the point of the sketch is lost if the arguments are not clearly presented; so pace and energy, though important, must not obscure the dialogue. It is not a sketch which works well in schools; it is best performed for that age group in an out-of-school environment, and best of all to a mixture of adults and young people.

The pupils' chairs are placed facing downstage and towards centre stage. The teacher's desk is similarly placed but on the other side. The pupils are waiting for the lesson to start; giggling, chattering, discussing last night's TV, etc. BRISTER *is deep in thoughtlessness.* MR FLETCHER *strides in looking rather the worse for wear. He bangs his briefcase on his desk. No one takes any notice. As he yawns and pulls himself together the class quietens down and looks at him expectantly.*

FLETCHER: Morning, everybody.
ALL: (*With varying degrees of sing-song lethargy*) Morning, Mr Fletcher.

FLETCHER: Right. Now. We're going to carry on this morning with our study of the staff room.

(*There is a small murmur of bafflement*)

CULSHAW: D'jer what, sir?

FLETCHER: (*Bringing out his joke*) Life in the Ancient World, Culshaw!

DOREEN: Oh, it's a joke.

CULSHAW: (*Reassuringly*) Must be Wednesday.

FLETCHER: (*Who hasn't heard or takes no notice*) Now, on Monday last we looked briefly at Christianity and the birth of Jesus of Nazareth. What did we discover about his actual birthday? Samantha?

SAMANTHA: (*Waking from her daydream*) Er . . . that he was not born in the year nought, sir.

(*The class is fairly surprised*)

FLETCHER: Yes. Good. We can't be sure when he was born actually, but it was almost certainly *before* the year nought, which of course puts a big question-mark over whether he was born at all. (*It takes a moment for this magnificent illogicality to sink into the class, but from this point begins* CULSHAW's *determined attack on* FLETCHER's *credibility*) Now, much more interesting from our point of view is the remnant of another belief, another philosophy – the Stoic philosophy, which we find . . .

CULSHAW: (*Hand up, excited*) Sir, sir!!

FLETCHER: (*Wearily*) What is it, Culshaw?

CULSHAW: Sir, there's a woman walking across the football pitch, sir!

(*The class is delighted at something of real interest but quietens immediately* FLETCHER *speaks*)

FLETCHER: (*Icily*) I am sure we are all indebted to Culshaw for his profound and helpful remarks on the peripatetic qualities of the female biped . . .

CULSHAW: But when was she born, sir?

FLETCHER: How the hel . . . (*Pulling himself together with dignity*) I have no means of discovering that, Culshaw.

CULSHAW: But that puts a big question-mark over whether she was born at all, (*Innocently*) doesn't it, sir?

(*There is a pregnant pause*)

FLETCHER: On page 46 we find a brief outline of Stoic philosophy. It was popular with many people. It is a fine belief – strong, stark, courageous . . .

CULSHAW: But was it true, sir?

FLETCHER: Culshaw, I am beginning to find these interruptions irritating. Was *what* true?

CULSHAW: What the Stoics believed, sir.

FLETCHER: I don't think I quite understand what you're getting at, Culshaw.

CULSHAW: (*Butter wouldn't melt in his mouth*) Sorry, sir. I just wondered whether they believed in strong stark courageous truth . . . or a load of noble codswallop – sir.

FLETCHER: (*Rescuing what he can from the situation*) Ah! So Culshaw knows what truth is! Well, well, well! Ladies and gentlemen of Year Eleven, this is an historic day . . .

CULSHAW: I dunno that I do know what truth is, sir. I just wondered if you did?

FLETCHER: (*Caught off guard*) Truth? Ah . . . er . . . well . . . truth is . . . ahem . . . truth is what is ultimately . . . um . . . something which . . . er . . .

DOREEN: (*Who looked it up last week and recites*) Something which outlasts fashions and civilisations and remains whether anybody cares about it or not.

(*Even* CULSHAW *is impressed.* FLETCHER *flounders*)

FLETCHER: Er, yes. Thank you, Doreen: well put. That's it. The unchangeable, the basis of the universe.

CULSHAW: (*Relentlessly*) So it wasn't true, then sir?

FLETCHER: (*Patiently*) What wasn't?

CULSHAW: (*Overreaching himself for once*) Stogie tism . . . stosket . . . what you said sir: them ancient beliefs.

FLETCHER: That would be a very rash assumption, Culshaw.

CULSHAW: (*Supported by the class*) No, sir! You said! If no one believes it any more, if it hasn't lasted then it can't be the truth.

ALL: Yeah. That's right sir. You said. Come on, Fletch. Etc, etc.

FLETCHER: (*Quietening them down genially*) Yes, yes, all right . . . in a way. But remember, my learned friends, there are many aspects of Stoic belief in that Christianity you're all so fond of. Of course it is the central core of Christianity that is so different *and* so difficult . . .

SAMANTHA: Sir, just 'cos it's difficult doesn't mean to say it's wrong!

FLETCHER: (*Bringing out his trump card*) Really, Samantha? Well, I should have thought that, if all men were supposed to believe and accept it, it should be extremely *easy* to understand.

DOREEN: Why do you say that about Christianity, sir?

SAMANTHA: Yeah, you don't say it about anything else.

CULSHAW: Things which you happen to know are true.

SAMANTHA: Things which *you* believe.

FLETCHER: Oh really? Such as what?

DOREEN: Well, arithmetic, sir, and technical drawing.

SAMANTHA: Biology.

BRISTER: Physics. (*There is a moment's pause as all turn to gaze at* BRISTER *with awe and wonder. Then back to the fray*)

SAMANTHA: Yeah, just because electricity is hard to understand, doesn't mean it isn't true.

DOREEN: Sir, you're always saying things need a bit of effort. (*And here she quotes him. The others join in as they recognise it*) Nothing great was ever achieved without hard work.

FLETCHER: (*He is embarrassed*) Yes, yes, yes, all right.

SAMANTHA: Well, there you are, sir. Why should it be different when it comes to learning about God?

FLETCHER: Well, I'll tell you, Samantha. You see, all the basic questions about physics, astronomy, geonomy, physiognomy and so onomy . . . er . . . so on, have been answered and, what's more, been proved to be true *by experience.* Now there are some very basic questions about God which cannot be answered.

CULSHAW: There are some very basic questions about cancer, sir, like how and why. But that doesn't stop people dying from it.

DOREEN: Sir, you said it was important to prove things by experience; well, there's a lot of people who have proved Christianity by experience. Why don't you believe them?

FLETCHER: That's very simple – I haven't had the experience myself.

CULSHAW: 'Ere, has Mr Fletcher ever been up in a rocket?

SAMANTHA: (*Wondering what he is getting at*) No.

CULSHAW: Ah, so he doesn't believe in space-travel.

DOREEN: (*Catching on*) Has he ever fallen under a tube train?

SAMANTHA: (*Enjoying this*) No!

DOREEN: So – he doesn't believe in electrocution then!

SAMANTHA: Hang on! Has he ever been to Greece?

DOREEN: Don't think so.

CULSHAW: Oh dear, so that probably doesn't exist either.

SAMANTHA: I wonder why he bothers to teach us about it?

DOREEN: It's awful when you think what he's missing.

SAMANTHA: Yeah, shame really!

DOREEN: I mean, he doesn't believe in the Indian Ocean, Battle of Waterloo, oxygen . . .

CULSHAW: Brain surgery, radio waves, childbirth . . .

DOREEN: Igloos, kangaroos . . .

FLETCHER: (*Who has had enough*) All right, all right, that'll do. This is all getting rather silly and the arguments are fatuous.

CULSHAW: (*Quickly*) Yeah, well they're all based on your reasoning, sir.

FLETCHER: (*Grasping his ear and giving it a tweak*) Look, Culshaw, you stupid little boy; I can read books, understand historical documents and believe what intelligent people tell me.

CULSHAW: Yeah. Always excepting the Bible, the Dead Sea Scrolls and the Archbishop of Canterbury.

FLETCHER: Yes. NO!! Um, that's different. It can't be proved.

DOREEN: Any more than anything else. Right!

FLETCHER: All right. OK. (*He is quiet and very much in control of his mounting impatience. But he's got them now*) You prove to me, you *prove* to me, that Jesus of Nazareth actually existed.

(*The room falls quiet as* CULSHAW *takes up the challenge*)

CULSHAW: You prove to me that your great-granny actually existed.

FLETCHER: Well . . . that's easy; I've got her birth certificate.

DOREEN: Forged.

FLETCHER: (*Disconcerted. He tries again*) And . . . and photographs. Plenty of photographs.

SAMANTHA: Fakes.

FLETCHER: (*With the quiet certitude of desperation*) Look, there are lots of people who actually remember her.

CULSHAW: (*Quietly but finally*) They're lying.

FLETCHER: I've got diaries!

ALL: Oooooh. Tut tut!

SAMANTHA: Very unreliable sources.

DOREEN: Subjective.

SAMANTHA: Biased.

CULSHAW: Emotional.

FLETCHER: (*Not even trying to remain calm any more*) Look, this is ridiculous! How can I prove anything if you constantly disallow the evidence?!

CULSHAW: (*With mock surprise*) Isn't that funny, sir? That's exactly what I would have said about Jesus. Oh – there is just one other thing I could bring up as proof, since you say things can be proved by experience.

FLETCHER: (*Pause. But he is interested despite himself*) Well?

CULSHAW: (*After a long pause, without removing his eyes from* FLETCHER) I've met him.

Getting Ready

WOMAN; MAN; TEENAGE BOY; VICAR; CHORUS; VOICE

Preparations for Christmas start earlier and earlier these days as the commercial machine starts winding itself up from mid-October. By the final week before the great day the pressure is enormous, frantic and obsessive: 'Did they send us a card last year? Whom have we forgotten? Where will everybody sleep? I've run out of icing sugar. I don't care whether she's a vegetarian, I'm not cooking two dinners! What on earth can we get Daddy on our pocket money?' Late on Christmas Day most of us collapse from a mixture of food and nervous exhaustion. Almost proverbially, the baby Jesus is excluded in the whirlwind of activity. But what if the risen Christ in all his glory were forgotten, too? Now read on.

Wherever 'RHYTHM' *is indicated, the four characters make up a human clock. If a larger choral group is possible, they create the clock behind the action and sustain the rhythm throughout the sketch, keeping the sound low through the spoken passages and high through the rhythm sections. The sound can be more sophisticated than the simple 'Tick-Tock' suggested here – a grandfather clock with a whirring chain and pendulum might be effective. When only the four characters are used, they re-form the clock between the dialogue. This can be worked out through improvisation. One solution is for the* VICAR *to represent the minute hands, starting at ten minutes to midnight; the* MAN *and the* WOMAN *to use their right and left arms respectively to create the continuous circle of the second hand as it ticks round. The sketch begins with the rhythm of the clock.*

RHYTHM: TICK-TOCK, TICK-TOCK, TICK-TOCK, TICK-TOCK.

ALL: It's Christmas Eve, it's Christmas Eve
And time is running out, is running out, is running out.

RHYTHM: TICK-TOCK, TICK-TOCK, TICK-TOCK, TICK-TOCK.

WOMAN: The pudding!

MAN: The presents!

BOY: The fairy lights!

VICAR: The sermon!

RHYTHM: TICK-TOCK, TICK-TOCK, TICK-TOCK, TICK-TOCK.

WOMAN: This year everything is going to be under control. My mother-in-law is *not* coming into the kitchen and there's going to be no nonsense over Camilla saying she's gone vegetarian! The dog is not going to sit in the cranberry jelly and dinner will begin well before the six o'clock news! If only I had time!

MAN: This year *I'm* looking after the Sellotape! There will be no arguments about the nauseating pink of the wrapping paper and every present will be clearly labelled and round the tree by midnight, not halfway through the Queen's speech! And this year Kevin will not be given a 'Changing the Guard' tin drum in his stocking! If only I had time!

BOY: This year the fairy lights are going to work! They are not going to flash on and off and then fuse for the whole of Christmas Day! Every bulb will be checked and wired up in sequence. We're not going to have the Royal Ballet on all afternoon, either! All the important programmes will be clearly marked with a red pen in the *TV Times*! If only I had time!

VICAR: This year I am going to preach a meaningful Christmas sermon! I will not have Darth Vader or a cuddly Care Bear in the pulpit, nor will I ruin my sermon notes with one of those dolls that wets themselves! I will think through everything beforehand and preach on the relevance of the birth of Christ to the modern world! If only I had time!

RHYTHM: TICK-TOCK, TICK-TOCK, TICK-TOCK, TICK-TOCK.

WOMAN: So much to do!

MAN: So much to wrap!

BOY: So much to fix!

VICAR: So much to say!

ALL: If only I had time!

RHYTHM: TICK-TOCK, TICK-TOCK, TICK-TOCK, TICK-TOCK.

(*The four characters increase their flurry of activity*)

WOMAN: Where's the stuffing?

MAN: Who's got the scissors?

BOY: Who's got the screwdriver?

VICAR: Where's that handbook to the Bible?

WOMAN: If only those carol singers hadn't scoffed all the mince pies!

MAN: Who bought this revolting pink paper?

BOY: Who trod on the fairy?

VICAR: My mind's a blank! I should never have had that sherry!

RHYTHM: TICK-TOCK, TICK-TOCK, TICK-TOCK, TICK-TOCK.

ALL: Hurry up, it's nearly Christmas!

WOMAN: I need a microwave!

MAN: I need the scissors!

BOY: I need a fuse!

VICAR: I need another sherry!

WOMAN: So much to finish!

MAN: So much to organise!

BOY: So much to mend!

VICAR: So little to say!

RHYTHM: TICK-TOCK, TICK-TOCK, TICK-TOCK, TICK-TOCK, TICK-TOCK, TICK-TOCK, TICK-TOCK, TICK-TOCK.

ALL: Two minutes to go!

RHYTHM: TICK-TOCK, TICK-TOCK, TICK- (*The rhythm stops abruptly. The clock is silent. The activity ceases*)

WOMAN: That's strange. The oven timer's gone off.

MAN: My watch has stopped.

BOY: The video's flashing.

VICAR: Why is everything so quiet?

(*Slowly they look around*)

It's daylight outside . . .

MAN: The whole sky is on fire!

WOMAN: The light is blinding!

BOY: What on earth – (*He freezes*)

WOMAN: What's happeni – (*She freezes*)

MAN: This is extraor – (*He freezes*)

VICAR: Impossi – (*He freezes*)

VOICE: (*Off*) The Son of Man comes at an hour you do not expect.

The Claims of Christ

HENRY, *a partner in a firm of solicitors*; CAROLINE, *another partner in the same firm*; RON, *a bricklayer from London*

On December 18th, 1981, the Daily Mail carried a bizarre item under the headline, 'Twenty "Christs" claim £30,000'. It read as follows:

> Twenty people are claiming to be Jesus and the rightful heir to £30,000 left in the will of religious recluse, Ernest Digweed. Mr Digweed was found dead four days ago in the tent in the living-room of his house in Portsmouth. The walls were covered in crosses. He also lived sometimes under piles of deckchairs. He left his entire estate to Jesus so that he would have some money if the Second Coming should actually occur. But until then Mr Digweed named the Public Trustees as executors and it is they who must decide whether any of the claimants is Jesus. They refuse to reveal the identities of the hopefuls though one is rumoured to be a steel worker from Sheffield. They will not say what the criteria are for checking each claim. An official said, 'We have politely acknowledged all claims. Usually people go away after a while or admit they cannot support the claim. If, however, there was a claim which appeared to be theologically sound, then it would have to be considered very carefully.'

The mind boggles at the idea of a waiting-room full of people posing as the Son of God. What clothes did they choose that morning? Did they come on the Underground? Swap parables while they were waiting? The whole thing is, of course, fantastic, not to say mentally deranged – an absurd pantomime in contrast with the awesome glory of the return of Christ as prophesied

*by Jesus himself. This sketch takes this newspaper article as
a starting point, but what interested us particularly was the
sentence, 'They will not say what the criteria are for checking
each claim.' How will we recognise Jesus when he comes? What
will happen on that momentous occasion? As it develops, the
sketch moves from farce into urgent discussion between two
agnostics. They suddenly find themselves facing an issue which
is of the utmost consequence to us all.*

*In order to prepare your audience for the shocking nature
of the beginning of the sketch, you may want to refer to the
article in the* Daily Mail. *To avoid upstaging some of the
comedy, we suggest that the introduction should go something
like this*:

> 'Twenty "Christs" claim £30,000.' Twenty people are
> claiming to be Jesus and the rightful heir to £30,000 left
> in the will of Mr Ernest Digweed, who was found dead
> four days ago in Portsmouth. He left his entire estate to
> Jesus so that he should have some money if the Second
> Coming should actually occur. Until then, Mr Digweed
> has named the Public Trustees as executors and it is
> they who must decide whether any of the claimants is
> Jesus.

A solicitor's office. CAROLINE *is seated behind a desk, upstage
left and* HENRY *is wandering around the room. Various papers
and books, including a Bible, are on the desk. There is a
second chair stage right.* HENRY *is in mid-conversation as the
scene opens.*

HENRY: I think we'll just have to wait on that one and
see how things go in the courts. (*There is a knock at
the door*) Come. (RON *enters in working overalls, eating
chips from a newspaper. They both ignore him*) Mind you,
with Harrison representing the other party, I doubt if we'll
have what you might call *a smooth ride*. (*He sniffs the air*)
Is there something cooking in here? Funny smell all of a
sudden.

CAROLINE: Hmmn. A distinct whiff of fried potatoes.

HENRY: Horrible. (*Turning to* RON) Sorry about the smell. Yes?

RON: I've come about the money.

HENRY: (*To* CAROLINE) Have we just had the windows cleaned?

RON: Thirty grand.

HENRY: Thirty what?

RON: Thousand nicker.

HENRY: I don't quite follow.

RON: Sorry?

CAROLINE: (*Pleasantly assuming control*) Shall we start again? You seem to be interested in some kind of remuneration.

RON: No, it's about the money.

HENRY: Whose money?

RON: Well, you've got it at the moment, but it's mine. You owe me thirty thousand quid. (*He parks himself in the empty chair*)

HENRY: (*With heavy sarcasm*) American Express all right?

CAROLINE: Is this anything to do with the Ernest Digweed bequest by any chance?

RON: Yeah, that's it, Digweed. That's the feller, yeah.

HENRY: (*Rather pointedly turning his back on* RON *again, he leans on the desk to talk to* CAROLINE) The Ernest Digweed bequest?

CAROLINE: Yes, this has become something of a problem recently, Henry. The late Ernest Digweed left a certain amount of money in his will –

RON: Thirty thousand pounds.

CAROLINE: (*Ignoring this*) And claimants have been flooding into the office ever since. This is number forty-eight.

HENRY: And who was this Mr Digweed?

CAROLINE: I don't know, really. He was found dead in a tent in the living-room of his home in Portsmouth.

HENRY: I see.

CAROLINE: He also made our company executors of his estate and occasionally lived under piles of deckchairs.

RON: Great man. Ahead of his time, you know, Digweed.

HENRY: (*Turning to him*) No doubt. So you are a relative of this Digweed, are you? (*His tone suggests that he hasn't yet forgiven him for the smell of chips*)

RON: Er, no.

CAROLINE: Digweed didn't leave the money to his family.

HENRY: Oh, I see. So he left it to . . .?

CAROLINE: Jesus Christ.

RON: That's me, yeah.

HENRY: (*After a brief silence*) Sorry, I'll ask that again. He left it to . . .?

CAROLINE: Jesus Christ, in case he should need ready cash on his return to this earth.

HENRY: A-ha. But if my facts are correct, Jesus Christ hasn't been around for a while, has he?

RON: Not until now, no.

CAROLINE: Though believers do expect him to return.

HENRY: And is that 'in clouds descending' or 'eating a bag of chips'? Sorry, I forget the exact wording.

RON: Well, it's figurative, isn't it?

HENRY: Yes, the main figure being thirty thousand pounds. I see. So, Mr . . .?

RON: Er, Christ.

HENRY: And your first name?

RON: Ron . . . er, Jesus, yeah. Ron's my second name.

HENRY: Your current address?

RON: Nineteen, Acacia Grove, Wapping.

HENRY: (*To himself*) A divine little suburb.

CAROLINE: Do you have any identification, Mr Christ? Passport? Driving licence?

RON: Not on me, no.

CAROLINE: Can you then perhaps in some other way substantiate your claim to be the King of all Creation?

RON: Well, it depends what you mean.

HENRY: (*Struggling to keep his patience*) All this red tape must seem rather strange and unnecessary to you, but you must understand that down here on earth there are certain formalities which we terrestrial beings must negotiate on our weary way.

CAROLINE: Can we get this straight? You have come along here this afternoon expecting to leave with a cheque to the tune of thirty thousand pounds because you claim to be the Son of God. Is that correct?

RON: I'd prefer cash. Fives and tens. Tax problems, you see?

HENRY: I would have thought Heaven was the ideal environment for tax exiles. Now look, this little question of identity *is* rather crucial to any settlement.

CAROLINE: Tradition has it, I believe, that your return was to be announced by the Archangel's Call and the sound of the Trumpet of God?

RON: (*Momentarily stumped*) Well, you wouldn't hear it from here. That was done over the Specific Ocean.

CAROLINE: (*Sharing a look with* HENRY) Also accompanied by the heavens passing away, the elements being dissolved with fire and the Earth and the works upon it being burnt up. But I imagine all this takes time.

RON: Once I've got the money I could arrange it, yeah.

CAROLINE: (*Humouring him*) It does sound rather expensive, yes, but these are the sort of things we would be looking for, you see? So, I think at the moment we shall have to file your claim under 'Pending' – pending the cataclysm. Good-day, Mr Messiah. (HENRY *shows him the door.* CAROLINE *smiles*)

RON: (*Clutching at any straw*) I've done a few miracles.

CAROLINE: The feeding of the five ducks?

HENRY: (*Escorting* RON *firmly by the elbow*) Yes, along with the healing of the slight headache and the miraculous draught of Guinness!

RON: (*Resisting*) I could do you a speech. A bit of moral teaching . . . 'Love thine anemones!'

HENRY: Not just at the moment, thank you. We're rather busy. (*Pushing him out*)

CAROLINE: Give our regards to Mr Digweed when you see him.

RON: He's dead!

HENRY: Exactly. I should think you and he get on rather well. (*Gives* RON *a final shove off*) My goodness me! I don't *believe* it! (*Rearranging his tie and generally recomposing himself*) I suppose we keep the money in an apocalyptic shelter while we work out the criteria for checking any claims.

CAROLINE: Very little legal precedent to help us, I'm afraid.

HENRY: (*Staring out of the window*) What would happen if the genuine article did walk through that door?

CAROLINE: It's hypothetical, of course.

HENRY: Of course.

CAROLINE: I didn't mean that. I meant that presumably there wouldn't be any door left to walk through.

HENRY: You're quite up on all this fire and brimstone stuff, aren't you?

CAROLINE: It's not the first time that the Bible's come to the aid of the legal profession. This case has prompted a little research, one way and another.

HENRY: (*Relaxing into the chair. He continues expansively, enjoying this theological whimsy for a moment*) So, what do you make of all this Second Coming bit, then?

CAROLINE: Seems to depend on what one makes of the first coming, really.

HENRY: (*Wagging his finger gnomically*) He's no easy man to impersonate!

CAROLINE: (*Seriously*) But would we know him well enough to recognise him if he did show up?

HENRY: Aha, yes. (*Suddenly perturbed by this idea*) That's a good point.

CAROLINE: And is he listening to us now discussing it?

HENRY: What? Oh, this is ludicrous! We can't seriously be discussing the return of a man neither of us believe in. It's absurd.

CAROLINE: But for the fact that we're holding his money. He might come back just for the money. We'd be the first to meet him. 'Hello, here's your cheque.'

HENRY: Well, he never showed any interest in money

before. Anyway, the fact that we're holding some money with his name on it doesn't make the possibility of his return any more likely. Does it?

CAROLINE: So you do regard it as a possibility?

HENRY: Ye . . . NO! (*Flummoxed*) I don't know. Give it to charity.

CAROLINE: (*Relentlessly*) But if we were wrong, we'd get it in the neck! We'd be singled out for divine retribution. (*Silence*)

HENRY: Look, this is silly! Forget it. Don't even *think* about it. (*He is obviously thinking furiously*) It's making me nervous.

CAROLINE: What about the money?

HENRY: Hmmn?

CAROLINE: (*Sharply*) Behind you!

HENRY: (*Whirling round to look at the door*) What?

CAROLINE: (*Laughing at him*) In the safe.

HENRY: (*Sighing with relief*) Oh. If it had Julius Caesar's name on it, would that mean that Julius Caesar was going to call round and pick it up?

CAROLINE: Julius Caesar never said he was going to come back, did he?

HENRY: (*Trying to reassure himself*) Look, Caroline, do you honestly expect me to believe that Jesus Christ is going to turn up here?

CAROLINE: (*Casually referring to her notes*) 'The Son of Man comes at a time you do not expect.'

HENRY: Who said?

CAROLINE: Jesus. Matthew twenty-four, forty-four.

HENRY: Ah, but that means he could come back at any old time. That's just to keep you on your toes.

CAROLINE: (*Perching on the front of the desk*) Even a conservative estimate gives him a fifty per cent chance of speaking the truth. Either he was or he wasn't.

HENRY: (*As if resting his case*) Take it or leave it.

CAROLINE: (*Reading from the gospel*) 'One will be taken and the other left.' (*Pause*) Fifty per cent chance there, too.

HENRY: (*After another pregnant pause*) Nervous?

CAROLINE: How do we know that either of *us* will be taken?

HENRY: Does the . . . um . . . does the Bible give any clues?

(Blackout. When this is not possible, they freeze)

GOD AND HUMOUR

Happy and abundant laughter is one of the most precious gifts that mankind has been blessed with by the Creator, who made man 'in his image'. Because of this, laughter on earth can be seen as a reflection of the laughter and joy which ring out eternally in Heaven. Of all literary forms comedy, with its implication of a happy ending giving meaning to all the disasters along the way, best portrays a truly Christian perspective on life. Dante's famous epic poem about the pilgrimage of a Christian soul was felicitously called *The Divine Comedy*. God has promised his people full redemption from sin and death and given to us a joyous hope of the eternal 'happy ending' in Heaven.

Christian joy is not just naïve escapism but is firmly based on the promise of God, and the promise is not just reserved for the future. James begins his letter by exhorting his brethren to 'count it all joy . . . when you meet various trials' (Jas. 1:2) and Paul was constantly saying things like 'Rejoice in the Lord always; again I will say, rejoice' (Phil. 4:4). This kind of joy should run deep, right to the core of our being. Although humour and its effect, laughter, cannot possibly express the totality of our joy, they are important evidence of this deeper spiritual reality. When the Israelites are brought back to their own land from exile in Babylon the psalmist describes the reaction of the people to the Lord's blessing: 'Then our mouth was filled with laughter and our tongue with shouts of joy' (Ps. 126).

There is clearly some distinction between the exultant laughter that bubbles up as a result of redemption and the equally God-given laughter of 'seeing the funny side of life', but as human experiences they are close cousins. What is strange is that Christians have often been afraid of laughter being connected in any way with preaching the message of redemption. If the message itself produces joyous laughter then it is appropriate that humour and laughter should sometimes be involved in the telling of it. This is not, in any sense, to undermine the message by mockery but rather to sharpen it with humorous illustration. One of the greatest English preachers, C. H. Spurgeon, was renowned for the way he often used humour in his sermons; it was in his nature to do so and was in no way contradictory to the gospel he preached. One could go further and say that if humour has a right place within Christian experience then it should be there as an 'enrichment' of life, and it is important that the 'riches' of the Christian life should be evident to others. Someone has remarked: 'The reason why there aren't more people going into church may well be the looks on the faces of those going out.' Of all people, Christians should be people who can be happy, who can laugh, enjoy the fun of living and even laugh at themselves.

The educational value of humour

As the different cycles of mystery plays developed, realism and humour were progressively introduced. As one might expect, this process began with the lowest characters in the overall hierarchy (the Devil, Herod, Pilate, Noah's unmanageable wife, the shepherds and the rogue, Mak the Sheep Stealer, the soldiers at the Cross) but gradually came to influence the conception of many other characters. As well as increasing the enjoyment for the spectator and commanding his attention and responsiveness more closely, this humorous realism was fulfilling a 'homiletic' purpose, namely to teach and warn people about the undignified and foolish ways of men. The book of Proverbs uses many comic touches for a similar purpose. The image of the sluggard, for instance, turning over in his bed 'like a door turns on its hinges' is meant to be funny and any dramatisation of that verse would also be funny. Far from diluting the force of the message, the humour in this case strengthens our understanding of the folly of sloth. In this way, satire which has a positive intention is a very useful tool for the Christian artist. However, satire can also be cruel and destructive, even in Christian hands (some of the more extreme writings of the eighteenth-century author, Jonathan Swift, demonstrate this). As an artistic device it needs careful control.

Remember that, in literary terms, humour and its uses within a Judaeo-Christian context, have been comparatively recent developments. It would be wrong to expect to find in the Bible, for example, an extended treatment of a comic theme, just as it would be wrong to expect to find a detailed discussion of the nature of physics. In English literary tradition there has always been a strong ingredient of comedy which has gradually changed as various types of humour have gone in and out of fashion. The figure of the 'Fool' or court jester in Shakespearian drama is one example, for here the figure of fun is also the voice of wisdom. The humorist is as memorable for his perception about human existence as for his witticisms. The Fool in *King Lear*, for all his buffoonery, is the only member of the court who is allowed to tell the king the truth. He does not flinch from his task, but he expresses himself in such a way as to call forth laughter as well as sorrow, and the truth is made easier to accept.

The profound implications of humour

It is just this very issue of the interplay between truth and humour that has helped one eminent sociologist nearer to faith in God in recent years. In his book, *A Rumour of Angels*, Peter Berger analyses the religious significance of humour. In essence, he argues as follows: anything that is comic depends upon a basic discrepancy or incongruity in order to be funny. This relates entirely to human situations (animals, for instance, are only comic when we view them as having human characteristics). The fundamental discrepancy from which all other discrepancies are derived is the discrepancy between man and the universe. The world is full of suffering, evil and death within which the human spirit is imprisoned. An appreciation of the comic puts this discrepancy into its right perspective and by laughing at the imprisonment of the human spirit, humour implies that the imprisonment is not final but will be overcome. This is quite different from many contemporary artists' and writers' notion of 'absurd laughter' in the face of a futile predicament. Humour, in this interpretation, is an intimation of redemption and can be seen as a religious vindication of joy. Such laughter points beyond the (often appalling) limits of the empirical world to the divine ordering and love of God.

Humour and the Christian sketch-writer

From the profundity of philosophical arguments one needs to come back to earth and consider more precisely the advantages that humour can have for the sketch-writer, and in particular the Christian sketch-writer. Firstly: entertainment. Every theatrical performance, *by its very nature*, involves elements of entertainment. With the predominance of television and films today, people live surrounded by entertainment and Christians need to learn the art in order to communicate. Jesus himself was a great entertainer ('he never spoke without a parable') and understood the importance of using this to capture people's attention. Laughter helps an audience to relax and register their involvement in the performance. A sketch can be weakened by too much self-indulgent humour, but if the main point of a sketch is always kept in view, various ingredients of entertainment along the way will assist in its communication. Jesus, very deliberately, described himself as a bridegroom at a wedding and, while the business of marriage is serious, the atmosphere at any Jewish wedding was full of festivity and enjoyment.

Secondly: we need to distinguish different types of laughter, in order to clarify our motives in creating it.

(1) *Sympathetic laughter*: There are many endearing things

about human behaviour which are simply funny and ought to
raise a laugh.

(2) *Laughter of recognition*: As an audience laughs at a
caricature or a situation, they laugh because they know it
to be true of themselves. The laughter has the effect of
educating the audience. Sir Philip Sydney, in the sixteenth
century, talked about poetry as a 'medicine of cherries', i.e.
something you enjoy which also does you good.

(3) *Nervous Laughter*: A psychological reflex to an embarrassing and maybe frightening situation. This can be the result of
ineptitude on the part of the dramatist, but it can also be an
indication that he is really hitting home.

(4) *Thoughtless laughter*: The Bible calls this 'levity'. It is an
idle kind of joking at something which isn't funny at all.

(5) *Mockery*: This kind of laugh intends to degrade and insult
whatever is mocked. It is the verbal equivalent of spitting.
Mockery also includes the laughter of disbelief.

In the story of Abraham and Sarah, the news of God's
promise of a son produces in each of them a different kind
of laugh, though the Hebrew word is the same. The Lord's
reaction to their laughter points up the difference. Abraham
laughs apparently with joy and amazement at the incongruity
of aged parents having a baby, but Sarah laughs to herself in
mocking disbelief, which she later tries to deny (Gen. 17, 18).
The story concludes with the safe arrival of the baby – a child
that symbolises God's covenant relationship with his people.
At the heart of this is the delightful 'joke' of ancient parents
conceiving a child. The baby is called Isaac; a Hebrew name
which means and sounds like laughter.

Humour at the heart
of God's communication to man

People quite often speak about God's sense of humour, not
irreverently, but in the context of the loving and gentle way
which God uses to guide and to teach us, to stop us doing

certain things and to help us do others. In his wisdom and with humour God appeals to *our* sense of humour and in a loving way the laugh is on us. When God communicates to Noah in one of the mystery plays he calls him 'my darling dear'; Noah, for his part, is overwhelmed with God's loving condescension and thanks 'the Lord so dear that would vouchsafe thus low to appear to a simple knave'. Such a discrepancy is comical, but at the same time profoundly sympathetic. It is in no way out of place, therefore, to discover some of the humour implicit in the background of the gospel narratives; in fact, there is probably a lot more humour than we realise. Because of the change in fashions over two thousand years we will never know for certain exactly what was funny to people in first-century Palestine. We are left with a few vestiges of humour which still make us laugh, or at least smile. From a probably very comic situation in the carpenter's shop, Jesus teaches us through the picture of the log and the mote: two men sawing a log, which slips off the bench. One man gets off lightly with nothing more than dust in his eye, but the other is unfortunate enough to receive the full force of the whole log. What is funny is that the man with a black eye tries to help the other with his speck of dust, even though he can't see straight. There is a cartoon element, too, in the striking contrast between the two debts in the story of the unforgiving servant. And surely there is humour in the actions of the four men who are so desperate for their friend to be healed by Jesus that they remove the roof of the house and lower him gently into the room, bed and all!

Some of these lighter touches in the Bible give immediate access to the deeper truths of gospel message. Twentieth-century men and women can see their likenesses in the people that surrounded Jesus, just as the following incident described by a woman on British television must have echoed the experience of so many blind people healed by Christ himself: this woman had the remarkable experience of being able to see, as the result of an operation, for the first time. One can hardly begin to imagine what an incredible experience this was. Amongst other first sights of things, there was the first time she saw herself in the mirror. She explained her horror at seeing this 'thing' sticking out in the middle of her face. 'My friends must have been keeping this from me for so long, and I never knew,' she said, but was later reassured when she saw that everyone else had a nose as well. It is natural for the sketch-writer to see in this ripe material for dramatising the story of Bartimaeus!

A Christian playwright, Christopher Fry, has said: 'Laughter is the surest touch of creation in man.' This, along with the statement by Søren Kierkegaard a century earlier, is a fitting summary of the issues raised here: 'The religious individual has, as such, made the discovery of the comical in largest measure.'

CREATING LAUGHTER

As we have seen in the previous article, there are many kinds of laughter. There are also many ways of creating laughter. A sensitive and discriminating approach is necessary for the Christian, as well as sound artistic judgement. Actors and writers concerned to explore this potential need to understand the elements of comedy, then to master the art of performance and finally to command the responsiveness of an audience. There is no substitute for experience, or for natural talent, and no limit to development – great performers find a lifetime too short to learn the art. Nevertheless, the following observations are intended to be an encouragement to learn from practice, rather than theory.

The elements of comedy

Incongruity: This is when something seems 'out of place' or does not normally relate to the other elements in the story. The Bible is full of examples – so much so, that one could claim that God's familiar means of communication to man is essentially comic: for instance, an ass talking to a prophet (Balaam), the youngest member of the smallest family of the least important tribe of Israel chosen to defeat the Midianites (Gideon), local shepherds in Bethlehem receiving the greatest visionary experience in history, the prodigal son given a lavish party (the parables of Jesus), a condemned criminal promised eternal life in Paradise. Although there is much more than humour in these incidents (and in many cases great dramatic intensity), the awareness of incongruity as an expression of God's condescending love makes them essentially joyful.

They contain the seeds of laughter. Most comic situations in the theatre depend on incongruity in some form or another. Careful observation of life, as well as a close understanding of the Bible, will furnish many examples.

Surprise: The best humour is frequently unpredictable – a door opens and a character appears who is supposed to be somewhere else; a stranger reveals her true identity; or – in the gospels – two disciples find they have been discussing the events of the passion with the risen Christ himself (the road to Emmaus). When the audience is genuinely surprised, or watches a character on stage being surprised by events, this will produce either laughter or dramatic tension, according to the context. Surprise of both kinds – audience and actors – is a crucial element in good writing, acting or directing, and is fundamental to theatre of all kinds.

Wordplay: This is one of the oldest elements of comedy and – when well exploited – delights the audience with revelations of double-meanings. The obvious form of this is the pun, and the Bible contains quite a number. Jeremiah, for instance, sees a rod of almond as a sign that God is watching over Israel but the Hebrew word used for the 'rod' and for 'watching' are practically identical, forming a memorable pun. Puns in excess can be very tiresome (notably in the youthful Shakespeare) but a great deal of modern humour is rooted in puns and double-meaning.

Reversals: When expectations are reversed, people will often laugh. For example, a famous epitaph reads: 'Here lies the body of Major James Brush, who was killed by the accidental discharge of a pistol by his orderly, 8th April, 1814. "Well done, good and faithful servant."' This is a total reversal of the accepted notion of a servant. Another reversal, inherently comic, is contained in the account of the blind man healed by Christ (John 9). His directness to the Pharisees and dogged conviction of his own healing put this beggar in a position of authority over the doctors of the law and they resent the implied reversal: 'You were born in utter sin and would you teach us?' Although this could be dramatised quite seriously, the character of the blind man and the naked irony of the story suggest strong comic potential (which does not preclude an overall seriousness of intention).

Deflation: This is one of the richest elements of comedy. A serious dramatic production is often vulnerable to accidental deflation, as when the heroine in *Tosca* flung herself from a tower in a suicidal leap, supposedly to land on a mattress out of sight of the audience, but was so heavy that she bounced up over a wall in full view of the auditorium. The net result was five minutes' hysterical laughter from an audience supposed to be witnessing a great operatic tragedy. Deflation, when used as a deliberate comic device, can function as a guardian of common sense. It can show pomposity to be ridiculous, or uncontrolled anger to be essentially absurd. One character can deflate the comments of another (see Clive and Roger in 'Party Games') or circumstances can show the folly of pretentiousness (see the fate of Goliath in 'David and Goliath'). In our own century, many forms of extremism – from religious bigotry to National Socialism in Germany – have been characterised by petty tyrants taking themselves intensely seriously. Humour in all its forms, from slapstick to mimicry to satire, can expose the ludicrous nature of such illusions and safeguard societies from fanaticism. It is such a powerful weapon that it needs careful aim, but it is fair to say that the true spirit of Christianity, characterised by joy, humility and self-sacrifice, has little to fear from deflation, whereas the lies of the devil are the most vulnerable target. Hell, it might be added, is a place where there is no sense of humour.

Recognition: This is when we see ourselves clearly mirrored in the comedy or recognise the accuracy of an observation. Mimics depend totally on this element in comedy, but in a broader sense it should be true of the characters and situations that we see on stage. For this reason, an audience will laugh more when they can relate to what is happening (children, for instance, will miss jokes about politics, whereas adults may well miss jokes about 'Gladiators'). If an audience recognises a 'type', or a certain kind of jargon, or a particular attitude, this will give the comedy greater plausibility and the response will be correspondingly enthusiastic (see section

below on 'commanding an audience'). Comedy goes wrong
most frequently when there is no point of contact.

The art of performing comedy

Timing: This is learnt by experience. In most cases an actor
should have silence and stillness for delivering a comic line,
but it should never be delivered too late. If the lines come
too slowly, a scene begins to become 'soggy', the pace slows
up, and the audience becomes strained. A line delivered too
fast, however, can sometimes be lost in the laughter over a
previous line, or 'upstaged' by somebody else's movement. It
cannot be emphasised too strongly that the instinct for timing
and the acquiring of great sensitivity to audiences and other
actors are the essence of comic performance.

Underplaying: 'Overplaying' comic situations is a disaster area
for amateur productions but, judging by the average television
comedy and more than a few repertory and West End
productions, the pitfalls are just as deadly to the professional
actor. If an actor gives too much emphasis to a comic line, or
smiles at his own witticisms, or laughs at other situations on
stage, he may well kill the humour. It is impossible to analyse
this without looking at each situation in turn but – generally
speaking – a 'deadpan' approach to comedy is often the best.
This is particularly true when the comedy is satirical and
depends on the characters taking themselves seriously. In
the case of obvious witticisms (when the character will know
that he is being funny) it is often better to 'throw away' the
line than say it with too much aplomb. This, however, needs
skill – for the line must be perfectly timed, well heard by the
audience and yet delivered as if it were a casual observation
just thought up by the character (not laboriously constructed
by a writer and then carefully rehearsed for three weeks). The
tradition of pantomime, when characters frequently deliver
their lines with great emphasis straight out to the audience,
encourages damaging habits for the aspiring comedy actor. It
is better to be as plausible and as natural as possible.

Characterisation: Much of the best comedy is produced by the convincing characterisation of a part – the way an actor walks, gestures, his mannerisms and inflections. Some actors develop this to such a fine art that audiences will laugh at 'who they are' rather than 'what they say'. Writers who create strong comic characters, and actors who live up to this challenge, will produce much more powerful comedy than is possible with a series of funny lines. Some playwrights who are naturally witty are often tempted to give all their characters the same gift of repartee – they cannot resist a funny line when they think of one. But a more subtle approach is to carefully study the drama from life, providing each character with a consistent language and appropriate reactions to each situation, above all allowing for the creation of unconscious humour when people take themselves too seriously. (In this case, it will often be the way a character misses the point, or fails to say something, that will be funnier than a conscious witticism.) In exactly the same way, an actor needs acute observation and strict self-discipline in the creation of a comic role. A mannerism, like a silly laugh for instance, can be very infectious, but over-used will alienate an audience. The actor should create entirely believable, subtle portraits of human beings, avoiding clichés such as professors who wander round clutching their lapels or telephone receptionists who continuously manicure their nails. Accurate observations of genuine idiosyncracies of behaviour lie behind the most memorable comic performances.

Expression: There are many ways of saying a line, and many modes of expressing joy, frustration, anger, hope. A supple use of the face, well-characterised gestures and voice control all add the vital element of credibility to comedy. Essentially part of characterisation, expression depends on accurate observation of how people react: a subtle performer will know how to say a line like 'Well, that's super, isn't it?' to imply, 'That's a complete disaster.' Technically, this may mean saying it too strongly, or saying the line absolutely expressionlessly, or letting the audience see some frustrated gesture (like screwing up a paper serviette) which goes in the opposite direction to the surface meaning of the line.

Good facial expressions will often make an audience laugh in anticipation of a line or a situation – always a sign that the comedy is working well.

Staging: An actor must always be positioned for maximum impact. In other words, he must not be upstaged if he is the central focus of the comedy. This does not mean he has to be downstage with all the other actors upstage, but it does mean that the audience's attention should be focused on him. Sometimes, it can add to the humour when an actor delivers a line from an unexpected position (under the bed, etc.). The important thing is for the director to avoid any visual distractions at the crucial moment.

Commanding an audience

This is the greatest challenge of all to the comedy actor. Even though every aspect of the performance is good, if the audience are not 'won over' the comedy will fall flat. The mood of an audience is a mysterious phenomenon. Audiences can vary in reaction enormously from one night to another – they cannot be made to laugh against their will (some just appear to lack vitality) but it is usually up to the cast to create the right atmosphere and, when this is achieved, an audience will respond gladly.

Seating arrangement: Audiences that are small and scattered round a large hall, often at too great a distance from the stage, will respond sluggishly. They should be seated close together, in reasonable warmth, and – ideally – suitable music should be played before a performance to create atmosphere and a sense of expectation. Obviously, if a sketch is performed during a service, the actors will inherit the mood of the previous half hour or so and care should be paid to the manner of the introduction and choice of the sketch. Congregations are a complex form of audience (especially when they contain elements that have not been expecting drama) and should be treated with great sensitivity – and never jolted too abruptly from a reflective to hilarious mood.

Punctual start: An audience that has been kept waiting for too long may be difficult to handle; a few minutes' grace for latecomers should be quite sufficient.

Contact: The clue to handling an audience is to understand that it has a personality of its own. This is sometimes dominated by a few people who may laugh at certain kinds of things more than others, but – despite the different elements – audiences tend to react as one. The secret, therefore, is to make contact with the prevalent mood in the audience – to appeal to the particular audience, to make friends. Audiences, like people, need to feel included; if they feel 'out of a joke' – or feel that the actors don't like them – the members of an audience will be inhibited. Affection is at the heart of good comedy. This implies a mutual response – the actors give and the audience gives back; as the actors give more to the audience and the audience becomes more susceptible to their charms, the audience laughs more readily and more infectiously as the performance develops.

It would be a fair summary of this article to say that a shared sense of humour is an expression of love, and the greater the love between the actors and the audience, the richer will be the comedy.

A NOTE ON SATIRE

The word 'satire' was introduced into the English language around the beginning of the sixteenth century, or a little before. During the Renaissance people rediscovered a penchant for classical literature and there they discovered that 'satura' was popular in ancient times. 'Satura' – literally a medley – was originally a verse satire in which prevailing vices and follies were held up to ridicule. One writer, Quintillian, claimed that the Romans thought of it first. Satire is, of course, no longer confined to poems; satiric prose was common in the eighteenth century and there has been much written for the theatre which could be called satirical. However, the purpose of this article is not to discuss literary evolution but rather to consider the nature of satire and its usefulness to the Christian writer.

How does it work?

As a literary means of denouncing, exposing or deriding folly, satire achieves this, in general, through a comic method. The devices of ridicule and exaggeration, distortion and caricature are often employed, even though the satire itself may have been initially provoked by a deep sense of moral outrage. Satire is a very practical form of writing and because it is political or social or moral in its objectives, it requires a wide readership. For satire to work, it relies on finding agreement with a significant proportion of its readership, whose laughter and enjoyment of the satire will shame those who are on the receiving end into renouncing the folly or vice in question. Occasionally, the horror of public exposure or the standing of the satirist will be sufficient to bring about the desired change, but usually widespread agreement expressed in laughter is necessary.

To agree presupposes sharing the same moral platform from which the satirist has launched his attack, since he can only be successful by appealing to a common standard of reasonableness, decent behaviour, wisdom, morality, virtue or common sense. That commonly respected moral platform is non-existent in our modern society, so there is little effective satire and what there is has little chance of appealing to a wide audience. What we often see today is an anarchistic kind of satire, where *everything* is made ridiculous (except the position of the satirist, of course); moral understanding has largely been eaten away, so little can be 'exposed'. Instead of pointing out the ridiculous *within* things, the ridiculous is overlaid *on to* them. The exercise becomes surreal or purposeless – the only objective being laughter itself, which is true of farce rather than satire. Some modern satirists have complained that, 'There aren't any sacred cows left.' That may well have been correct, but, of course, the one sacred cow left to be satirised is the position of the satirists themselves, the island of their own self-esteem and the folly of living in a world where nothing is sacred.

What are the dangers?

The main danger for the satirist is *arrogance*. By using his skill to pull down to size or to expose, he must pass judgement on other people and their actions, but if he uses his power to put himself on a pedestal, then he, too, must be pulled down. One way for the writer to avoid this danger is to base his satire on an authority higher than himself.

Another danger for the writer is to see satire as a *weapon* with which to inflict as much damage as possible. An angry man holding a weapon can lose his head and turn a piece which sets out to be corrective into something which is downright malicious. If the satire is too coarse (too exaggerated, too distorted, too absurd) it will risk missing its mark. Effective satire is sharp but often subtle.

Some cartoonists, for instance, are so vicious that their caricatures not only suggest that, for example, a particular politician is a corrupt monster, but also that the imagination of the artist himself is warped. Reactions which are over-extreme discredit themselves. On the other hand, satire may also miss its target by allowing the humour to cloud the 'serious' issue, instead of revealing it.

Finally, there is the danger of *mockery*. Whereas satire arises from the feeling that something important is at stake, and should imply a concern for the best interests of the people involved and the issues raised, mockery does none of these things.

Satire and the Christian writer

A Christian writer should, first of all, be alive to the dangers outlined above, but then he should carefully assess the likely response to his satire, particularly over issues where his authority is most liable to be questioned. In these instances satire may not be the wisest approach. Although the Christian is strongly warned against making spiritual judgements about his fellow human beings on his own authority, at the same time he is called to be salt in the world, to fight evil, to encourage others in wisdom and maturity and to share his understanding of truth; this can only be done on the authority of God, otherwise it would be presumptuous. It is also interesting that all these aspects of a Christian's calling correspond closely with satire; the one difference appears to be the issue of laughter, and making things look ridiculous. Does God give us the authority to do that? The answer given by the Bible is 'yes'. Apart from the many instances of satirical teaching spread throughout the Bible (e.g. about the Fool or the Sluggard in Proverbs), we are told clearly on several occasions that 'God scorns the wicked . . . He who sits in the heavens laughs; the Lord has them in derision . . .

The Lord laughs at the wicked, for he sees that his day is coming.' At times, God's attitude to man's sinful folly appears to be satirical.

There is a penetrating and very funny piece of satire in Isaiah. In a general way, over several chapters, Isaiah is expressing God's feelings about the idolatry that the Israelites have fallen into while they have been in exile in Babylon. This crystallises in a sustained piece of satire in verses 9–20 of chapter 44, in which the absurdity of worshipping blocks of wood is spelt out. In order to get through to the exiles, the prophet needed a strong, rational approach, coloured with humour, which would knock the *status quo* of idol-worship. The result is effective.

It is clear, then, that God's Word endorses the use of satire; the Christian writer must be equally clear that God would endorse his *motives*. God's attitude to mankind is characterised by unending compassionate love; he disciplines waywardness also out of love and he urges us to speak the truth only in love. This was the way Jesus corrected people and was his underlying motive even when he was attacking the hypocrisy of the Pharisees with stern invective. Love did not prevent him from using strong words; it gave him a reason to use them. As Jonathan Swift wrote about himself,

> Yet malice never was his aim,
> He lashed the vice, but spared the name.

The Christian satirist has a very important role to fulfil but he will only be successful if he tries to understand the feelings of God, if he expresses himself with sharpness, wit and good humour, and if he always retains a sense of his own weakness and a healthy attitude to his own foibles. Swift also said,

> Satire is a sort of glass, wherein beholders do generally discover everybody's face but their own.

A Christian satirist should try and have regular inspections of his own face.

Warm-Up Joke

FRONT OF HOUSE MANAGER, *a dedicated servant of the local theatre*

Something has gone badly wrong with the start of the show. There is an embarrassing hiatus followed by a heated argument in the wings. The audience are aware of this without being able to make out all the details. With an aura of self-conscious importance, the FRONT OF HOUSE MANAGER *clambers on to the stage from the auditorium. He gives a tight smile to the audience and disappears into the wings. There is another suppressed argument. A brief struggle ensues. Something rips. The* FRONT OF HOUSE MANAGER *is shoved back on stage. As he turns to face the audience, his throat dries up and one side of his face suddenly develops a nervous tic.*

MANAGER: I am here to warm you all up with a joke. Apparently this is the best way to warm people up. 'Tell 'em a joke, that'll warm them up.' So this is what I am going to do. I'm going to tell you a joke. (*Pause*) I should say that this isn't the kind of joke that's *guaranteed* to warm an audience up, but it's a fairly ordinary joke which I'm rather banking on. (*Pause*) There's about a twenty-five per cent chance that this joke may fall completely flat. But anyway, let's look on the bright side of things – even if you don't laugh, I may have successfully warmed you up. (*An overlong silence*) One should, of course, be able to remember jokes. But I find that at times like this all kinds of jokes are rushing through my mind, except the one I'm wanting to tell, which right now has slipped my mind. (*He begins to rummage through various pockets*) Had I not taken the precaution of writing it down, this would be a serious setback as far as warming you up with a joke goes. (*He searches frantically, finally pulling out a whole wedge of papers, keys and coins which fall on to the stage.*

On hands and knees, he sorts through this rubbish. At last he holds a crumpled piece of paper aloft in triumph. He laughs nervously and tries to recover some composure) Ah, here it is. (*Straightening it out*) This will really make you smile. It may even make some of you laugh. I don't know. I was certainly very amused myself when I heard this particular joke for the first time. (*An anxious look out at the audience*) There is, of course, a slight possibility that some of you *may* have heard this joke before. In which case you will laugh, not a happy-go-lucky, thoroughly-warmed-up sort of laugh but a rather hard, sarcastic laugh, followed by an awkward silence. (*There is one and he fills it with an embarrassing laugh-cum-snorting sound*) Anyway, I'm sure you're wanting to hear this joke, whatever it is, so without further ado, I will read you the joke. (*He suddenly checks himself with another thought*) I hope you will forgive me for reading it, but I tend to stumble over some of my words, particularly some of the important ones such as the lunchpine, er, punch . . . punchline. (*He is sweating*) It's worse of course, isn't it, when you stumble earlier in the joke so that by the time you get to the punchline no one knows what on earth you're talking about!! (*There is no reassuring response from the audience*) Anyway. The Joke. That is, assuming I can find my glasses. Ah, here we are. (*He smiles as he finds them surprisingly easily, but he jabs himself in the eyeball as he puts them on. Eventually he finds a handkerchief to dab his weeping eye, now closed tightly shut*) 'Read on, noble Caesar!' (*Pause*) That wasn't a quote actually, but it's a fair bet that someone did say that to Caesar at some point in his career. It – (*He chuckles*) er, it may even have been when he was trying to warm the Senate up with a joke!! (*He laughs alone*) I don't know. Anyway, hopefully not the same one as this. The Joke (*Reading from his piece of paper*) Now, there were eight pounds of potatoes and two pounds of sugar and a large packet . . . (*Desperately, he turns the paper over. The joke is nowhere to be found. Silence. Vainly he looks to the wings for help. None is forthcoming*) I have a feeling that my wife has got this joke somewhere in Tesco's right now. (*Thinking hard*) So look, if I don't come back, you'll know she hasn't got the joke. (*Pause*) She . . . um . . . she never *did* get the joke actually! Ah! That was quite a funny joke I made just then, wasn't it? But . . . probably *not* funny enough to warm you up, so I will try and find the other one if I possibly can. (*Exit at great speed*)

Party Games

EMMA, *glittering hostess at a cocktail party*; ROGER, *her husband, amiable but faintly boorish*; JOANNA, *a fashion-conscious friend of* EMMA'S; CLIVE, *a self-assured dilettante*, JULIAN, *a debonair art historian*; DAVID, *a morose friend of* ROGER'S *and a drag on the party*.

'Party Games' is a satirical sketch, looking at four aspects of behaviour: the first, with the tennis commentary, is the social competitiveness of two women; the second, with the rugby commentary, is intellectual one-upmanship; the third, with the boxing commentary, is the sparring relationship of a husband and wife; and the fourth and most serious, with the cricket commentary, is the social taboo surrounding the subject of death. Each scene takes place with a different combination of characters at a cocktail party. The sketch is really a set piece – perhaps one half of an evening's performance – when performed in its entirety. However, Riding Lights have frequently performed just the tennis and rugby sequences (as in their revue Colour Radio *on the Edinburgh Festival Fringe) or the tennis, rugby and cricket matches, without the boxing match. More or less any combination will work, though one section does not normally stand on its own. The inclusion of the cricket match may be dictated by the overall emphasis of the evening. Sketches like this, which do not touch on religion directly but explore familiar attitudes, are immensely valuable in a group's repertoire. They appeal to the more sophisticated elements in the audience as well as, hopefully, inspiring a healthy recognition of the evils satirised. However, 'Party Games' needs careful rehearsal and good timing to work well. Directors should feel free to stage the sketch imaginatively without slavishly following these recommendations. The heart of the material is in the handling of the commentaries and we would suggest all the men in unison as tennis umpire,* DAVID *as rugby commentator,* CLIVE *as boxing commentator, and* JULIAN *as cricket commentator. The*

*choices may depend on the actors' ability to imitate appropriate
TV commentators. Naturally, additional actors could be used
for the commentaries but there may be dramatic advantages in
restricting them to the guests at the party. If the latter is done,
the guests should 'come out of character' in order to do it and
– most important – the other characters should not be aware of
the commentators (in other words, not look at them or respond
to them). As for the verses after each section, this is a question of
taste. If the tennis and rugby matches are performed alone, then
only the verse after the rugby match should be recited to 'round
off' the sketch. If the whole sketch is done, the verse after the
cricket commentary is essential (and implies at least one other
verse being used earlier). The action of the cocktail party goes on
throughout, but great care should be taken to avoid upstaging
the main focus of action. The way to do this is to arrange the
characters not involved in a sequence to chat silently upstage,
with the minimum of movement.*

EMMA *spruces herself for the arrival of the guests.* ROGER
*wheels on the drinks trolley. The doorbell rings and one
by one the guests arrive:* CLIVE, JULIAN, DAVID. *Improvised
greetings – 'Clive! Long time no see!', 'What can I get you,
David?', 'Julian, me old hearty!' General social laughter and
pleasantries. The men chat together, except for* DAVID *who
pensively munches cheese biscuits by the trolley and pours
himself the first of several whiskies.* JOANNA's *voice is heard
offstage: 'Cooee!' She enters.*

EMMA: Joanna!
JOANNA: Emma. Darling!
EMMA: You sweetie, how super of you to come!
JOANNA: I could hardly refuse such a fabulous invitation card.
    It's had pride of place beside my Louis-Quatorze clock.
UMPIRE: Love-fifteen.
EMMA: Really? I didn't know you had a Louis-Quatorze
    clock.
JOANNA: I didn't know you could do such beautiful italic
    writing, darling. It must have taken you an age to write
    out every card.

EMMA: They were printed.

UMPIRE: Love-thirty.

JOANNA: No! I could have sworn . . . Clive, how are you, and Roger, and Julian, what a pleasant surprise! Emma, you've got together a super crowd of people.

EMMA: It wouldn't have been half so good without you, Joanna, you look fabulous.

JOANNA: Thank you.

EMMA: You can wear absolutely anything and look fabulous. These days I daren't risk anything off the peg, I'd look hideous.

UMPIRE: Fifteen-thirty.

JOANNA: Oh come on, Emma, I don't think you look a day over forty-five.

UMPIRE: Fifteen-forty.

EMMA: I feel it, honey . . . I feel as if I've been dragged through a hedge backwards when I look at you – how on earth do you manage to keep so slim? . . . Talking of slimming, how did the health farm go?

UMPIRE: Thirty-forty.

JOANNA: Fine, darling, thank you.

EMMA: Did the brutes put you on a starvation diet?

JOANNA: Actually, when they saw how I looked, they told me that I didn't need the deep treatment and I was allowed to feed extremely well.

EMMA: (*Removing some succulent pastries*) Well, dear, you won't want to risk one of these on top of all that food – how about a Ritz biscuit?

UMPIRE: Deuce.

JOANNA: It's quite all right, darling, I've just been told to avoid *real* cream.

UMPIRE: Advantage Mrs Baxter.

JOANNA: Oh, by the way, I've brought you a bottle of wine. (*She hands it to* EMMA)

EMMA: Darling, how thoughtful . . . Mmmm . . . (*Looking at the label*) You really shouldn't have bothered . . . These Spanish wines are such fantastic value for money, aren't they?

UMPIRE: Deuce.

JOANNA: Yes, they're super.

EMMA: (*Kissing her*) Honey, thank you.

JOANNA: Oh, I forgot, there's a card to go with it – that's for Richard for passing his maths A level.

EMMA: Five pounds . . . Joanna, you shouldn't have . . . Actually, I'm told it was the toughest competition for ten years.

JOANNA: Really? Well, in that case, you must be thankful that he had the experience of the previous three attempts.

UMPIRE: Advantage Mrs Baxter.

EMMA: Talking about previous attempts, I see you haven't brought that super young chap from Lloyds with you tonight. Is it all off?

UMPIRE: Deuce.

JOANNA: Yes.

EMMA: Pity, I thought he was just your type. Anyway, your husband must be fairly relieved.

UMPIRE: Advantage Mrs Forsythe.

EMMA: (*Moving over to* JULIAN) You have met Julian, by the way, haven't you?

JOANNA: Well, of course, he won't remember me.

JULIAN: No, I'm afraid I don't.

EMMA: But I was sure you knew each other – the way Joanna spoke about you on the phone last week, you sounded like an old friend . . . Now, who is everybody going to have – er, *what* is everybody going to have, I should say – Julian, Joanna . . .?

UMPIRE: Game to Mrs Forsythe.

ALL: Play up, play up and play the game!
   The object is to stay on top.
   And keep your neighbour on the hop.
   Play up, play up and play the game!

ROGER: Talking of *art*, Clive, I find a lot of fifteenth-century Italian art bores me to death.

CLIVE: Such as?

COMMENTATOR: He's tackled.

ROGER: Well, to be honest with you, Clive, even a lot of the Sistine Chapel ceiling bored me.

COMMENTATOR: But it's out to the fly-half.

CLIVE: I'm sorry, I thought you referred to fifteenth-century Italian art.

ROGER: Did I? Ah.

COMMENTATOR: Thrown forward. Scrum down.

CLIVE: The Sistine Chapel ceiling was painted from 1508 to 1512, but presumably your guide book told you that when you last visited Rome . . . Actually, when did you last visit Rome, Roger?

COMMENTATOR: He's got possession.

ROGER: Oh . . . It was before the war, of course, I can't remember exactly.

CLIVE: Ah, I understood you were some sort of expert on art.

COMMENTATOR: And it's out down the three-quarter line, going for the corner flag.

ROGER: I wouldn't say expert . . . I just know what I like, you know. I'm a great fan of Leonardo, as a matter of fact.

CLIVE: Which paintings of Leonardo had you in mind?

COMMENTATOR: Up and under.

ROGER: Well, the *Mona Lisa* for one thing.

CLIVE: And?

ROGER: And many of the others, of course.

CLIVE: Of course.

COMMENTATOR: He's racing down the wing.

ROGER: What about yourself?

COMMENTATOR: But a beautiful bodycheck from the full-back.

CLIVE: Me? Oh, I didn't say I was a fan of Leonardo.

COMMENTATOR: Knocked on. Scrum down.

CLIVE: No, I'm very partial to the later extravagances of Giulio Romano.

COMMENTATOR: A dramatic break down the three-quarter line.

CLIVE: Mannerism has a perverse sort of appeal to me.

COMMENTATOR: Lovely dummy scissors.

ROGER: What is Mannerism, exactly?

COMMENTATOR: Look at that high tackle!

CLIVE: Mannerism . . . well . . . it's a period in Italian art isn't it, Roger . . . about the time of Michelangelo . . .

COMMENTATOR: He's struggling on, about twenty yards to go.

ROGER: I mean, who are the Mannerist painters, other than Giulio Romano?

CLIVE: Um . . . aah . . .

COMMENTATOR: No, he's down and the ball's knocked into touch. Line out.

ROGER: Ah, well, I thought you were supposed to be our brilliant art expert.

COMMENTATOR: Not straight, a penalty kick. And now look at the concentration as he takes that kick.

CLIVE: Bronzino's *Cupid and Psyche* in the National Gallery, of course, is a fairly good example of Mannerist painting.

COMMENTATOR: And what a kick!

CLIVE: I find Parmigianino somewhat extravagant, but then Pope-Hennessy's discussion of Michelangelo's *Last Judgement* explains a great deal of familiar Mannerist motifs.

COMMENTATOR: It's a try, it's a try, what a text-book try; straight through those defences like a knife through butter.

ROGER: You studied art, did you?

CLIVE: No, I'm a civil engineer, actually.

COMMENTATOR: What studied coolness as he prepares for the place kick.

ROGER: Well, I've got to hand it to you, Clive, you know quite a bit about art on the quiet.

COMMENTATOR: Look at the ball sail straight over the bar and between the posts.

ROGER: I know who to get my information from about Mannerism!

COMMENTATOR: A perfect conversion. (JULIAN *walks over to* CLIVE)

JULIAN: I've been thinking – haven't we met before?

COMMENTATOR: Just a few more minutes of injury time.

CLIVE: No, I don't think we have.

JULIAN: I'm sure I saw you this morning flipping through one of my catalogues on the Mannerist exhibition at the National Gallery.

COMMENTATOR: He's in trouble.

CLIVE: Er, you wrote the catalogue on the Mannerist exhibition?

JULIAN: That's right.

ROGER: Well, if you're interested in Mannerism, you should talk to Clive, he knows all about it.

CLIVE: Er, well . . .

COMMENTATOR: The forwards are just piling into that loose ruck . . . He's in really serious trouble.

ROGER: Clive could knock anybody into a cocked hat when it comes to Mannerism – one of the most knowledgeable people in the country.

JULIAN: Really? It's strange I haven't heard about you.

COMMENTATOR: Scrum five and they're going for the shove over.

CLIVE: (*Fumbling for a distraction*) Um . . . (*Seeing* DAVID *pouring himself another whisky*) Joanna, you've been very quiet this evening!

COMMENTATOR: It's out to the fly-half.

CLIVE: Have you met this fellow Julian?

COMMENTATOR: He's kicked for touch. And it's all over, and what a nail-biting performance it was.

ALL: Play up, play up and play the game!
The object is to keep your cool,
And make your neighbour feel a fool,
Play up, play up and play the game!
(*They all raise their glasses*) Cheers! (*Hubbub of conversation*)

EMMA: Now, what would everybody like to drink? Clive?

CLIVE: A gin-and-it wouldn't go down amiss, thanks.

EMMA: Super. Roger, can you organise a gin-and-it for Clive? (EMMA *and* ROGER *exchange comments, heard only by the* COMMENTATOR, *as they move around the room, talk to the guests and offer drinks*)

ROGER: We're right out of gin.

EMMA: But I put it on the list.

ROGER: The off-licence was closed.

EMMA: You mean, you forgot to go to the off-licence.

ROGER: Are you saying I'm a liar?

EMMA: That's for you to decide, honey.

COMMENTATOR: And in the red corner it's Mrs Forsythe, and in the blue corner it's Mr Forsythe.

EMMA: And another thing, our bedroom looked like a bomb had hit it at six o'clock. You know perfectly well I use it for people's coats.

COMMENTATOR: A swift punch to the chest.

EMMA: Julian, is everything shipshape?

JULIAN: Yes, I'm working my way through these cheese biscuits, they're really divine.

EMMA: That's fabulous, darling. (*To* ROGER) I suppose it was too much to ask that you might have done something for a change, like clear it up?

COMMENTATOR: He's got to watch that stinging right-hander.

EMMA: Joanna, can I get you a refill?

JOANNA: That's terribly sweet of you, I'd love one.

EMMA: (*To* ROGER, *who is picking up a vol-au-vent from the table*) Don't stand there stuffing yourself, get out and talk to people.

COMMENTATOR: She's running rings round him.

ROGER: They're your friends, I don't see why I should talk to them.

COMMENTATOR: He's ducking out of trouble.

EMMA: I don't have to remind you that it was your idea to have this party? But, of course, if I hadn't sent out the invitations nobody would ever have got one.

ROGER: Well, I . . .

COMMENTATOR: She's caught him on the wrong foot.

EMMA: (*Between her teeth, as she smiles at* CLIVE) You're utterly selfish, Roger.

COMMENTATOR: He's taking a lot of punishment.

EMMA: Clive, I'm so thrilled you could come, now what will you have?

CLIVE: Well, I'm rather partial to these, actually.

EMMA: Good, so long as you're enjoying yourself, that's super. (*She sweeps past* ROGER)

ROGER: I suppose you think you're Coco Chanel or somebody, do you – wafting all over the place?

COMMENTATOR: A borderline low punch, there.

ROGER: Well, let me tell you, you're making an ass of yourself at this party.

COMMENTATOR: A dramatic come-back, he's obviously intending to go the full distance.

EMMA: Joanna, I must introduce you to Clive, he's absolutely fascinating.

JOANNA: I've been dying to meet him.

EMMA: You'll get on terrifically well. (*To* ROGER) The only ass in this house is you, standing around making a total fool of yourself, tossing off wildly inaccurate statements about subjects you know nothing about.

COMMENTATOR: But she's right back in there, pummelling away his resistance.

EMMA: Couldn't you see that Clive was vastly more intelligent than you?

COMMENTATOR: She's going for the early knockout.

EMMA: No, you couldn't. You're probably slewed out of your mind.

COMMENTATOR: The whiplash blow to the forehead.

EMMA: When I meet people like Clive and Julian, I sometimes wonder why I married you.

COMMENTATOR: He's out for the count.

ROGER: Do you regret marrying me?

COMMENTATOR: One, two . . .

EMMA: Frankly, yes.

COMMENTATOR: Four, five, six . . .

EMMA: If it wasn't for the children –

COMMENTATOR: Eight, nine . . .

EMMA: I would have left you years ago.

COMMENTATOR: Ten. He's out.

EMMA: Julian, can I possibly tempt you to one of these banana boats?

JULIAN: Emma, it's really very good of you and Roger to do all this, you know.

EMMA: Oh, the pleasure is ours, we absolutely revel in it.

ALL: (*With conspicuously less panache than before, they raise their glasses*)
Play up, play up and play the game!
Never tiring, never sagging,

Keeping on, though spirits flagging,
Play up, play up and play the game!
Cheers . . .

EMMA: Now, David, how are you managing?
You've been frightfully quiet this evening.

DAVID: I've been feeling a little down, actually . . . the wife
. . . you know how it is . . .

EMMA: How is she, the poor thing?

DAVID: Not . . . um . . . not too good, you know how it is.

COMMENTATOR: She's getting a lot of movement off the
pitch, but he's not going to take any chances with this
attacking field.

CLIVE: Cheer up, old chap, she'll pull through all right – see
if she doesn't!

COMMENTATOR: There's the googly.

DAVID: Thanks, Clive, but I don't think she will this time,
the doctor says . . . It's a matter of time, really.

COMMENTATOR: But he steers it backward of square and he
gets two.

EMMA: I must send her some flowers.

DAVID: It's kind of you, Emma, but she's not conscious, so
she won't appreciate them.

COMMENTATOR: Just pitched it too wide there.

JOANNA: Could I take the children for a few days? I could
take them off to the country, down to Lulworth Cove – it's
so beautiful. I've got a cottage near there. Do you know
Dorset, Clive? I think the south coast is fabulous at this
time of year.

COMMENTATOR: Clive comes in past Umpire Buller.

CLIVE: Yes, actually, I often have holidays on the Isle
of Wight.

JOANNA: Really?

DAVID: The trouble is what to do with the children in a few
months' time.

COMMENTATOR: Just fell short of third slip, but he's digging
himself in.

DAVID: You know, I keep wondering what to do when –

EMMA: Would everyone like some coffee?

DAVID: When it's all over . . . after . . . after Amanda's –

EMMA: Now, David, will you have some coffee?

COMMENTATOR: She's probing round the off stump.

DAVID: I mean, after Amanda is dead.

COMMENTATOR: But he's hooked it for six!

CLIVE: Good heavens, look at the time!

ALL: OWZAT!

DAVID: It's only half-past nine.

CLIVE: So it is.

COMMENTATOR: No, he's put it down.

DAVID: Dead. I can hardly believe it. Dead . . .

EMMA: Coffee, coffee!

DAVID: Do you think death is the end, Roger?

COMMENTATOR: That's a super shot. That'll be four.

ROGER: Oh, I've been near to it many times in the war, you know . . . funny thing, war . . . Actually, I was in the Royal West Kent Regiment for a short spell – time of my life. Shan't forget that in a hurry.

COMMENTATOR: Wide.

DAVID: I keep asking myself, what's the point of all this? I mean, it's not just the fact that Amanda is going to die, it's just the thought that we'll all be dead in –

EMMA: David, isn't it hospital visiting time? We shan't mind a bit if you have to nip off.

COMMENTATOR: A beautifully flighted off-break.

DAVID: Actually, she's in the intensive care unit, I wouldn't be any help. No, it's the thought that death comes to us all . . .

CLIVE: Did you know that you can have four men standing on an ostrich egg without breaking it?

ROGER: Good heavens.

EMMA: I can't believe it.

CLIVE: No, really.

ALL: OWZAT!

COMMENTATOR: No ball.

DAVID: Dead . . . Do you know what that means? This body, this magnificent instrument, reduced to a shell.

ROGER: Look, for heaven's sake, old chap – don't go on and on.

EMMA: You've got overtired, we all understand. I've got

your things here – and I honestly think that you'd benefit from a good night's sleep. Here's your coat.

ALL: OWZAT!

COMMENTATOR: She's bowled him. Bowled him middle stump and he goes away towards the pavilion, shaking his head.

DAVID: But I keep thinking – any of us could die tomorrow, we could die in our beds tonight!

CLIVE: Look here, think of the ladies, David.

DAVID: Joanna, do *you* think death is the end?

JOANNA: I think . . . I think I'd like another drink.

DAVID: I could go out in my car now, any of us could go out in our cars now, straight down the main road and crash into a lamp-post.

EMMA: David, please.

CLIVE: This is hardly cricket, old chap.

DAVID: Suddenly, that's it . . . shutters . . . wham . . . that's it.

ROGER: What you need is a good, stiff drink. Here now, play the game, David. Drinks all round, Emma, Joanna, Clive, Julian.

ALL: Play up, play up and play the game!
We'll play it to our final breath
And never, ever mention d—
Play up, play up and play the game!

Thought for the Day

The RADIO PRESENTER, *in this brief (and pointless) interlude between sketches, can be male or female. The image is of the middle-class, middle-aged Radio 4 contributor from the Home Counties. Sympathetic, comforting, a quiet, earnest presenter of* Thought for the Day. *Many such contributors are ordained, so clerical garb is a possibility, but a tweed jacket for the man and twin-set and pearls for the woman fits the classic image. (If the PRESENTER is a woman, the reference to 'shaving' can be replaced by 'powdering our nose', etc.)*

The PRESENTER sits down at a desk, with a microphone. He/she smoothes the script, breathes deeply. Ideally, a red light glows to indicate a recording in progress.

(*Softly, intimately*) We all ask the question 'Why?' (*Smiling, amiably, gently*) Why is there so much suffering in the world, so many unanswered questions. 'Why?' Why must we put up with this? Why is this happening to me? Why is this moron boring me to death for an excruciating one and a half minutes? Yes . . . (*emphatically*) why is *Thought for the Day* so long? And *so* infuriating? (*Another sweet smile*) Why do people – we all experience this – talk down to us, imagining that somehow they are a superior species with a special insight into the meaning of life, and the audience are a load of mindless imbeciles? Why this appalling suffering? It's sometimes hard to come to terms with the enormous pressure of those boring seconds, which can cruelly interrupt our day at the very moment we feel a sense of happiness and well-being. One moment we are shaving, or singing in the shower, the next patronised, bored, our intelligence insulted, deeply depressed. (*Now more serious and urgent*) How can we *possibly* deal with all these raging emotions? It often seems that the Bible has no answers, and this is perfectly

true, because when the Bible was written, the radio had
not been invented. (*Pause*) Faced with the anguish of
our times – the unprecedented onslaught of pious idiots
trying to talk chummily to us as if we were Mr and
Mrs Average – what can we do but vomit uncontrollably
into the basin which only a minute before was swishing
happily with soapy water? So, today . . . why not give a
thought to all those who have to listen to others giving
us a thought? Good morning.

Urban Madness

DR HUGHES, *a psychiatrist*; CHRISTOPHER, *his patient*; MICK, DAVE, *shop assistants*; DR HAMILTON, *consultant psychiatrist*.

If there is a profoundly spiritual message in this sketch, the authors would be grateful to hear about it. So far, we have not been able to find one but we would like to keep our minds open. After all, if many sermons are carefully planned to be full of subtle nuances and deep insights but, in fact, turn out to be banal and pointless, presumably the reverse is possible. This sketch, which has been carefully devised to have no hidden depths whatsoever, may change many lives. However, there is no evidence for this attractive hypothesis and so far this piece has only caused a few members of the audience to change their trousers.

The stage area is divided into two: a consulting room in a psychiatric hospital, and a hardware/auto accessories store. The two environments can be very simply created. The original Riding Lights production had two chairs for the consulting room and a worktop table with a few tools scattered around for the store. If lighting is available, then the consulting room can be lit in an intense pool of light, with the rest of the acting area in darkness – losing this light in favour of the hardware store during the flashbacks. It may be useful to have a couch for the psychiatric patient – a classic accessory for someone being taken on a journey into a traumatic memory – but rehearsals will dictate whether the tension needed in the patient and the need for quick transitions will benefit from this. The two shop assistants should wear oily overalls, and the consultant psychiatrist a white coat. In a fully lit and theatrically staged performance, it may be possible to double up the parts of Dave and Dr Hamilton – it can add an extra frisson of insanity.

Although there is no purpose or deep meaning in a revue sketch like this (first performed on the Edinburgh Festival Fringe, along with 'Party Games' and 'Warm-Up Joke', in the Riding Lights revue Colour Radio) *it can perform a function along with more serious material. 'Urban Madness' can set up the theme of living in the modern world, the rage inside so many people today, or it could open a conference session on counselling. It is probably unsuitable for an evangelistic rally or a funeral service.*

DR HUGHES *is seated in his consulting room.* CHRISTOPHER *enters, carrying a large wrench which he conceals under his jacket.*

DOCTOR: Hello, Christopher, how do you feel this morning?

CHRIS: Not . . . good. (*He carries a large wrench which he keeps concealed*)

DOCTOR: Oh dear.

CHRIS: Oh dear. BAD!

DOCTOR: Oh dear.

CHRIS: Oh dear.

DOCTOR: Now, this morning, Christopher, we're going to carry on with our journey back into the past to find out what it was that made you go and do what you did. You were a nice, gentle . . . what have you got there, Christopher?

CHRIS: Mine!!

DOCTOR: What is it?

CHRIS: Socket . . . socket and . . .

DOCTOR: And . . .?

CHRIS: Wrench.

DOCTOR: Well done. A wrench. Now tell me, Christopher, how did you come to be holding that wrench in your hand when it happened?

CHRIS: Shop . . .

DOCTOR: Shop. Let's go back to the shop.

CHRIS: No, no!

DOCTOR: You must.

CHRIS: Man, serving me . . . (*Man comes in behind counter*)

DOCTOR: What did you ask him for, Christopher?

CHRIS: Wrench.

DOCTOR: And he found nothing strange about this?

CHRIS: No. Normal. Everything normal. Wanted it for car
. . . just making enquiries . . .

   (*Crossfade to shop on stage left*)

CHRIS: Good morning. I wonder if you can help me. I want
some tools for a repair job on the car.

MICK: Take yer pick, sir.

CHRIS: Well, the thing is, I'm a bit of a novice at this sort of
thing, and I'm rather keen to get the right stuff.

MICK: Know what yer mean, sir. Take yer time, sir.

CHRIS: I don't know what you'd recommend. Apparently I've
got to get at the brake drum which I assume is on the
back wheel.

MICK: 'Ubnut.

CHRIS: Sorry?

MICK: 'Ubnut, sir.

CHRIS: Hubnut, ah, yes. Well that could be it. Now what the
garage was talking about was a 36 millimetre socket and
wrench.

MICK: Thirty-six millimetre, sir?

CHRIS: Yes.

MICK: Volksy?

CHRIS: Sorry?

MICK: 'Ave you got a Volkswagen, sir?

CHRIS: Yes! Yes I have!

MICK: They're the only ones that do 36 millimetre. It's not
a standard make.

CHRIS: Not standard. That's a pity. So I suppose you
wouldn't have such a thing as a 36 millimetre socket and
wrench?

MICK: Depends whether you want the half-inch drive or the
three-quarter inch drive.

CHRIS: Ah, drive. What exactly is that?

MICK: Sometimes they only make the half-inch for some of
them, sometimes only the three-quarter inch for some of
the others.

CHRIS: I see. So the main thing is not to land up with a
half-inch drive wrench when you've got a three-quarter
inch socket. Right?

MICK: Right, sir. But you can get a converter.

CHRIS: A converter.

MICK: Converter unit.

CHRIS: I see. Well, what can I get in the way of converters?

MICK: Well, you can get a three-quarters to a half or a half to three-quarters.

CHRIS: So if I ended up with a half-inch drive wrench but a three-quarter inch drive socket, I could get a converter for that?

MICK: That's right sir. Or else you could do it the other way round.

CHRIS: Have you got one?

MICK: What?

CHRIS: The lot.

MICK: I haven't got a converter, sir. No converters of any description.

CHRIS: I see.

MICK: Got a wrench for you, sir. (*Placing it heavily on the counter*)

CHRIS: Ah, well, that's a start. Now this is definitely what I need, is it? I mean, I'm told there's a lot of pressure in that sort of department . . . brake drums and so on.

MICK: Oh yeah, sir. A lot of pressure there, sir. 'Ere, Dave! You got a Volksy, aincher?

DAVE: Yeah, that's right.

MICK: What do you use to get yer 'ubnuts off wiv?

DAVE: Not one of them for a start. Bend as soon as look at it. Smash to smithereens. No good at all.

CHRIS: Well, look here, what sort of thing do I need?

DAVE: Well. Dunno. Difficult job. See there's 24 'undred pounds of pressure on there. I seen people with one o' them. You get a wrench like that. You get a great lump of scaffolding on the end of it . . . three great big blokes leapin' up and down on it . . .

CHRIS: Wouldn't that . . . er . . . do something to the tool?

DAVE: Oh yeah. You'd get some gouge marks in it, yeah.

CHRIS: Just the gouge marks?

DAVE: Probably smash it.

CHRIS: Um . . . how much is this wrench?

MICK: Twenty-four pounds ninety-nine.

CHRIS: Fine, Well, I'm not sure I can really commit myself to the idea of this wrench . . .

MICK: Well sir, you take yer time. We're 'ere. We got the time. We got the sockets, we got the wrenches, we've got three-quarter inch drive, half-inch drive. You can take yer pick.

CHRIS: How about a 36 millimetre socket?

MICK: No, sir. Not the 36 millimetre *socket*. There's not a lot of call for them; they're only on Volkswagens.

(Chris goes temporarily beserk. Crossfade to psychiatrist's)

DOCTOR: It's all right, it's all right! Remember. You kept your temper; no man could have been more patient. You went back.

CHRIS: No!!!

DOCTOR: Yes. You decided to ask for some other things on your shopping list. Some screws. Christopher, you must face up to those screws. Now, you left aside the thought of buying a wrench.

(Crossfade back to shop)

CHRIS: Look, tell you what. Let's forget about the wrench altogether. There are one or two other things on my list. Screws. What I'm after is a three-quarter inch zinc roundhead No. 8.

MICK: Three-quarter *roundhead* zinc?

CHRIS: Yes.

MICK: You definitely wanted the roundhead, sir?

CHRIS: Well, yes.

MICK: Got a three-quarter inch black . . .

CHRIS: Not the zinc?

MICK: No sir, not the zinc. We can do you a half-inch zinc. Got a half-inch zinc countersunk.

CHRIS: Not the three-quarter inch zinc roundhead?

MICK: No. I got them in black.

CHRIS: Well . . . look, what about a white hook? I just want one . . . about an inch long, and a thread on the end to screw into things with.

MICK: A *white* hook, sir?

CHRIS: If you've got the white.

MICK: I've got a yeller, that's close!

CHRIS: That's not quite the point.

MICK: Brass. That's the same thing, but it's not got the white cover.

CHRIS: Look, I just want one small white hook, one inch . . .

MICK: Hey, Dave! Got any one inch white hooks?

DAVE: You mean them things they had before the war with the thread on the end? Don't make them any more, sir. I doubt if you'd find one of those screws anywhere in London. Possibly in the north of England . . .

CHRIS: Polystrip.

DAVE: Poly what, sir?

CHRIS: Strip. Polystrip.

MICK: Got some Polyboard.

CHRIS: I . . . I've already got the board; you see I've sawn through the boards and I want something to put on the end of them.

MICK: Hasn't it got something on the end of them already, sir?

CHRIS: On . . . on the . . . on the side, but not on the end where I've sawn through . . .

MICK: What was that?

CHRIS: Polystrip!!!

MICK: What's it like?

CHRIS: Well . . . it . . . I suppose it comes in those little plastic packets . . . it's about three-quarters of an inch wide . . . with . . . and it's long . . . and . . . I don't know!!

MICK: Got some of this Polystrip, have we, Dave?

DAVE: Yeah, there's been a big run on that. Polystrip. I'm almost sure we haven't got any left. People are using quite a bit of Polystrip these days.

CHRIS: Drawing pins!!!!!

MICK: Now they're very popular. We're expecting some in at any moment. There's a brass one here which is a bit rusty, and there's a grey plastic-covered one which is a bit bent.

DAVE: You could straighten that out on the lathe, no trouble.

(*Chris clubs them to death maniacally with wrench*)
(*Crossfade back to psychiatrist's*)

DOCTOR: It's all right, Christopher. It's all over now. That's it. No more. You couldn't take it any more.

CHRIS: What have I got, Doctor?

DOCTOR: It's hard to tell.

CHRIS: Paranoid schizophrenia?

DOCTOR: I doubt it. Possibly obsessional schizophrenia, catatonic schizophrenia. We've certainly got psychosomatic schizophrenia here.

CHRIS: I was told I had paranoid schizophrenia.

DOCTOR: Dr Hamilton?

HAMILTON: (*Entering*) Oh no. Possibly paranoid paraphrenia, but you won't find paranoid schizophrenia anywhere in this hospital. Possibly at the Warnford in Oxford. We could, of course, do you a clinical depression, they're very popular! (*Chris raises wrench. Blackout*)

The Lethe Lectures: Amnesia

LECTURER

The human memory is one of the most mysterious functions of the brain. It can completely block out traumatic experiences, mercifully casting an entire course of lectures at theological college into total oblivion, for example. It can arrange the forgetting of awkward tasks and repeatedly wipe out hundreds of requests to pick up a pair of socks from the floor. But this gentle anaesthetic function which nature has thoughtfully provided can wreak a spectacular revenge on anyone involved in public life or in a lecturing ministry. One of the most famous telegrams must be the message from the writer G.K. Chesterton to his wife. He had arrived to deliver a talk and his telegram read simply: 'AM IN MARKET HARBOROUGH WHERE I OUGHT TO BE?' This is every lecturer's nightmare, though admittedly it may be a dream come true for their audience. One of the authors of this book was halfway through a rhubarb crumble in a university staff canteen when informed that the YMCA down the road was packed with people waiting to hear him deliver a lecture. His memory was of a similar consistency to the half-demolished dessert on the table, as he had no recollection of agreeing to give the lecture or any recall of its title or subject matter. This sketch is a tribute to those remarkable individuals who actually remember to be in the right place at the right time and to speak on the right subject. Until, of course, in front of a packed auditorium their minds go a complete blank . . .

Enter LECTURER, *depositing sheaves of notes on to lectern.*

Tonight, my subject is the mental health problems of rural clergymen in 1922 – no, I'm sorry, that was yesterday. Tonight, of course, my subject is 'Amnesia'. Amnesia. Many things are brought to mind by a subject like Amnesia. It haunts its victims like a . . . like a . . .

like the problem that it is. Anyone who has experienced
this disease commonly known as . . . this awful predicament which in layman's terms is known as . . . Now,
perhaps one of the greatest unexplained factors in the
death rate of Cornish clergymen in the early 1920s is
the massive number of – sorry? Yesterday? . . . Did
I? I must apologise, of course, my subject for tonight
is . . . Sorry, I've just lost my place in my notes. It's
Amnesia, of course! Over thirty per cent of patients
suffering from this curious affliction – and thirty per cent
is a large proportion – over thirty per cent of amnesia
sufferers are suffering precisely because . . . the other
seventy per cent are in such a similar predicament. (*He
looks round awkwardly*) The layman will talk, often quite
casually, of a 'mental relapse', or the writer, perhaps,
might talk of a 'writer's block', whereas the actor may
well talk of . . . (*He receives a prompt*) of 'drying'. All
these aspects – the 'mental relapse', the 'writer's . . .
problems', or the actor who . . . who wonders what the
next words are . . . all these are, in miniature, forms of
. . . (*He receives a prompt*) Amnesia. John Keats aptly
sums up the experience of Amnesia with the words of
his poem 'Ode to a bird': (*Reciting quickly*)

> My heart aches, and a drowsy numbness pains
> My sense, as though of hemlock I had drunk,
> Or emptied some dull opiate to the drains
> One minute past, and Lethe-wards had sunk.

(*He gives a short laugh of relief*) Perhaps only Shelley
could have expressed it so beautifully. He refers to
'Lethe', the famous river of forgetfulness, one draught
of which can cause total oblivion. (*Long silence . . .
then emphatically*) What *is it* . . . about . . . Amnesia
that presents . . . (*Silence. He bites his lip*) two of the
greatest challenges to the patient? The first is, the
person cannot remember why he came to the doctor
and so cannot give him the slightest indication of his
problem. The second is, the person cannot remember

why he came to the doctor and so cannot give him the slightest indication of his problem. 'The rest is silence', in the words of the greatest poet and dramatist in the English language – sorry, I'm terrible with names – the fellow with the beard, a little pointy beard . . . bald head and a – (*Gestures to his neck*) – what do you call them? The bard! The bard. William the Bard. That, I think, wraps it up for tonight, although it might be added that Prussian military ambitions were evident, of course, in the Balkans. Tomorrow we'll enjoy a complete change of subject when I'll be discussing Amnesia.

(*Exit confidently*)

APPENDIX ONE

The Bad Samaritan

VICAR; MAN; ROBBERS; PRIEST; LEVITE; GOOD SAMARITAN; SPECTATOR

The title of this sketch is self-explanatory. It was written to illustrate how not to write and perform sketches and has been staged exclusively in seminars on creative drama. Needless to say, it should not be performed in a service of worship or in any context where it would undermine the credibility of other sketches. It could be performed for fun in the context of a church party or rag concert, but any misplacing of an 'off-beat' item like this could well lead to all-night prayer meetings in the church for the salvation of the drama group. The discussion points for seminars are printed in bold type.

A curtain conceals the backstage area. Assorted scuffling sounds, dull thuds and ripping noises signify the presence of the actors waiting to begin. The VICAR *walks onstage from the auditorium. He coughs.*

VICAR: I'd like to give you all a very warm welcome to the Hallelujah Drama Effort from St Botolph's and - (*Nervously glancing over shoulder to see if they're ready*) – they've come all the way from Spillingham today – (*Looking round again*) – and I imagine . . . (*Whispering off*) Are we ready to go? (*Beaming unctuously*) Er, in a moment or two, they'll be presenting a tableau which many of us will find, I certainly speak for myself here, many of us will find a real source of spiritual encouragement.

BAD INTRODUCTION

VOICE ONE: You stupid idiot!
VOICE TWO: Ssh!!

VICAR: And so, without further ado, I welcome the, er, (*Glancing at leaflet*) Hallelujah Drama Droop . . . er, Group, I should say, from St Botolph's. (*Exit. Pause. He re-enters*) I've just been asked to say that this is a dramatic rendering of the parable of the Good Samaritan. (*Exit*)

DELAYED START

(*Enter* MAN *who wanders around aimlessly. Silence. He whistles*)

MAN: I hope there aren't any *robbers* round here. (*Pause*) There were certainly *robbers* around here last time I walked from Jerusalem to Jericho. (*Pause*) *Robbers* have been known to beat people up. (*Pause. He is desperate*) Listen, hooves!

BAD CUES

(*A large quantity of robbers descend on him instantly and beat him up for a very long time. Pause*)

ROBBER ONE: Hey, let's beat him up.

ROBBER TWO: Yeah. (*They beat him up again for a very long time*)

OVER-ACTING

ROBBER THREE: Well, let's get on the horses and go.

ROBBER FOUR: Horses?

ROBBER THREE: (*Stage whisper*) He said he heard the sound of hooves.

ROBBER FOUR: What did he say that for?

ROBBER THREE: I don't know. Come on. (*He jumps on* ROBBER FOUR'S *back.* ROBBER ONE *jumps on* ROBBER TWO'S *back*) Giddyup. (*Exeunt, galloping*)

TROUBLE CAUSED BY IMPROVISATION

(*Pause. Re-enter* ROBBER ONE)

ROBBER ONE: Hey, let's get out of here, there's someone coming. (*Exit*)

CLUMSY LINKING

(MAN *lies groaning.* PRIEST *enters reading a scroll and trips over him.* MAN *groans because he is really hurt*)

'REALISM' OF THE WRONG SORT

(*Exit* PRIEST *and re-enter* ROBBER ONE)

ROBBER ONE: Hey, quick, let's get out of here, there's somebody else coming. (*Exit. Awkward silence. Injured* MAN *gets up and looks for* LEVITE)

GOING OUT OF CHARACTER

(*Enter* LEVITE, *struggling into costume. He delivers a completely inaudible speech*)

BAD DICTION

(*Enter* ROBBER ONE)

ROBBER ONE: Hey, quick, let's get – (*He collides with the* LEVITE, *who is on his way out. Exeunt in confusion*)

BAD STAGING

(*Enter* GOOD SAMARITAN, *his hands outstretched in an awkward gesture of goodwill*)

GOOD SAMARITAN: Oh no! . . . Oh God, I have such a little to offer this man, but what I have I will offer him.

HACK SENTIMENT

MAN: Who are you?

GOOD SAMARITAN: I'm the Good Samaritan.

MAN: Where are you from?

TOO LITERAL

GOOD SAMARITAN: Samaria.

MAN: Samaria?

GOOD SAMARITAN: Yes.

MAN: But – But

GOOD SAMARITAN: (*Kneeling beside him*) Come, I will pour this oil on your wounds. (*He searches in vain for the prop, which he has left backstage. He mimes pouring oil*)

BAD STAGE MANAGEMENT

MAN: I don't know what to say.

GOOD SAMARITAN: (*Producing script*) Here.

MAN: Thank you. (*He reads*) Oh, I am so glad you have come. I was walking down the road to Jericho, when I was set upon by robbers and they beat me up and I was lying here and first of all a priest passed by on the other side and then a Levite passed by on the other side and then you came and – (*Realises speech has finished*) – then you came.

UNNECESSARY VERBIAGE

GOOD SAMARITAN: It's all right now, you'll be safe.

MAN: (*Kneeling*) Oh God, you've saved me. (*He stretches out his hands, inadvertently poking a finger up the nose of the* GOOD SAMARITAN *who is kneeling behind him. The two actors are joined by the rest of the cast, who sing a song involving the word 'happy' at least seven or eight times. This is to illustrate* **CRINGE FACTOR**. *Further embarrassment is provided by the* GOOD SAMARITAN *who steps forward after the song to address the audience*).

GOOD SAMARITAN: We'd like to talk to anyone who's been interested in this play and would like to know more about its message to stay around for coffee and just a chat. There is a bookstall which you're very welcome to read and thank you again for having you with us. Er . . . So anyone who would like coffee at the back afterwards, would they come to the back afterwards.

SPECTATOR: (*Coming up to the* GOOD SAMARITAN)
Excuse me, hello, I'm David Stephenson – I'm a drama teacher and I thought there might be one or two ways in which you could improve that sketch.

GOOD SAMARITAN: But we prayed about it.

SPECTATOR: I still think that –

ROBBER ONE: Look, we had an all-night prayer meeting about that sketch.

SPECTATOR: Well, I only wanted to suggest –

ROBBER TWO: Are you saying we haven't got faith? (*The actors jostle the* SPECTATOR *threateningly*)

SPECTATOR: No, no . . .
      (*Exeunt*)

                              FAILURE TO TAKE CRITICISM

APPENDIX TWO

The Riding Lights Membership Scheme

*If you want to support Riding Lights Theatre Company you can
become a Member of Riding Lights and*

BE PART OF THE VISION . . .

The vision of Riding Lights is:

To provide high quality theatre productions both new and
classic communicating a truthful understanding of life
To reach a broad audience with work of lasting value
To reawaken a strong dramatic tradition within the Christian
community and to affirm the presence of Christ within the
professional theatre

Over the past eighteen years, Riding Lights Theatre Company has grown from a small community project in York into
a significant UK touring company, bringing a wide range of
innovative theatre productions to thousands of people each
year as well as reaching a considerable international audience
through occasional tours, radio broadcasts on the BBC World
Service and the widespread overseas sales of books such
as this.

Riding Lights Theatre Company was formed when a
group of professional actors and writers were given practical support by a local church with a radical approach
to its role in the community. Initial finance came from
the generosity of a few individuals with a clear calling
to support the vital contribution that artists can make to
the character of our society. Since then Riding Lights has
been a pioneer in reinstating theatre as a powerful means

of Christian communication in a world dominated by the visual media.

Its early hallmarks of comedy and innovation caused it to be hailed as 'Christian theatre with a difference' (*Church of England Newspaper*, 1978). Concentrating on new writing and an ensemble style of theatre, the company's work has stretched far beyond the lightning biblical sketches for which it was originally famous; its productions have ranged across the theatrical board from street theatre to classic plays. Satirical revues have won awards at the Edinburgh International Festival, educational shows have been devised for schools, new full-length plays, sketches and musicals have been performed not only in some of the UK's premier theatres and on national television and radio, but in venues as diverse as universities, cathedrals, factories and prisons. Riding Lights has been on and through many different stages; many individual artists and technicians have played their part in its creative success; but also, most significantly, many other people have provided the ongoing practical support to keep this work and this vision alive during a time when so many other companies have disappeared.

The realities of funding such work took a new direction in 1992 with the launch of the *Riding Lights Membership Scheme*, which in its first two years has been joined by over 800 people. In a way that would have been impossible without such enthusiastic and committed support, the company is gaining increasing independence from other funding bodies and the freedom to plan its programme into the future. The support of Members has brought about a resurgence of the primary vision of the company, outlined in the statement above. Working in three different spheres – community theatre, regional touring and mainstream productions – Riding Lights is reaching (at the time of this publication) a theatre audience of 180,000 people every year, many of whom would not go regularly to the theatre, let alone to church.

Within the first two years of running the Membership Scheme, a number of new developments have been realised. The Riding Lights Roughshod company, our community theatre operation based for weeks at a time on local churches around the country and serving multifarious venues from the sublime to the ridiculous, has become so well established that two Roughshod companies are now be working simultaneously. In addition, there has been a highly successful regional tour of a play by Murray Watts, our first major prison tour, the commissioning of three new productions, eleven residential theatre courses, the creation of radio, television and video programmes, as well as the hosting of many theatre training days and workshops for churches and organisations nationwide. In 1992, Riding Lights received a Templeton UK Project Award (one of the most prestigious religious awards in the world) 'for enabling audiences to hear the gospel gladly'. All of this work has been undergirded by the generous support of the Members of Riding Lights.

Time and time again the company has proved how effective theatre is in reaching the parts which other forms of Christian communication fail to reach. In the present climate of social fragmentation and the increasing isolation brought by electronic media entertainment, the company's work is needed more than ever. We cannot do this on our own. We continue to seek a widening network of people contributing creatively, prayerfully and financially to establish the increased vision which we believe that God has given us. Can we invite you to become part of this vision?

The membership partnership brings to Riding Lights an informed, enthusiastic nucleus of support across the country, championing our cause in the community. Each supporter is a vital link with the needs of our audiences and a creative resource for new ideas. In return, we offer you a Membership card and information pack about the current state and programme of the company, a quarterly Members' Newsletter, advance booking opportunities at discounted prices, free participation in Members' workshops and seminars, as well as the possibility of meeting with other members in your area for feedback sessions, prayer groups and backstage visits. We want our members to become as fully involved in the life of the company as they are able or would wish to be.

We invite all our members to make a commitment to give on a regular basis to Riding Lights Trust (Registered Charity

No. 507803) at whatever level is appropriate for them. No contribution is too small or too large, as long as it is regular. Initially, we have been seeking to find 2,500 members whose contribution might average £5.00 per month. With this level of support, Riding Lights Trust would be able to fulfil its target of funding two Roughshod companies and providing support for Riding Lights Theatre Company's intended programme of two regional tours of new plays and two mainstream productions each year.

If you are interested in becoming a Member of Riding Lights, or in receiving further information, please write care of 'The Best Time to Act', P.O.Box 223, York YO1 1GW.

We believe that God is giving us the faith and the means to respond to a passage in Isaiah that has propelled us forward in recent years:

> Enlarge the place of your tent, stretch your curtains wide. Do not hold back; lengthen your cords and strengthen your stakes. For you will spread abroad to the right and to the left and your descendants will people the desolate cities.

. . . with your help we will continue to develop this vision.

Paul Burbridge (Artistic Director) and
Murray Watts (Associate Director)
Riding Lights Theatre Company
June 1995

UP TO DATE

Steve Turner

The bestselling collection of Steve Turner's most popular poems, including two of his earliest books, *Tonight We Will Fake Love* and *Nice and Nasty*.

'His verse is sharp and in focus; as vital as newspaper print and just as difficult to get off your hands.' Bono of U2.

'At last a poet who captures today with all the flair of a rock number.' Peter Lewis, *Daily Mail*.

During twenty-five years performing his own poetry, Steve Turner has given readings in Europe, Russia and America. His rock criticism has appeared in *The Times* and his travel writing in *The Independent*.

THE KING OF TWIST

Steve Turner

The *King of Twist* is Steve Turner's fourth, sparkling collection of poetry, combining the immediacy and humour of his earliest books with a sharper, more mature vision. In these poems he takes on the fears and pressures that threaten to lead us into a dull conformity and explores the 'wise madness' that offers a way out.

'Steve Turner's poems should be printed on bus tickets, beermats, matchbox labels, on giant hoardings across the city. They are gentle slogans for all the causes he believes in.' David Ward, *New Musical Express*.

'He is, underneath the sugar-coating of pop-art, a moralist, who undercuts the complacencies of right and left wing assumptions alike . . . He sees the skull beneath the comfortable skin.' D. M. Thomas, *Times Literary Supplement*.

A GIANT'S SCRAPBOOK

Stewart Henderson

A Giant's Scrapbook is a most arresting collection of poetry, a kaleidoscope of images observing life and love in the late twentieth century. 'Giant' is Henderson's quizzical and loveable spokesman for anyone who has ever felt restless or out of place in a world which does not seem to fit. Whether sarcastic, lyrical or witty, the poems communicate a yearning for personal wholeness and oneness with God in a fragmented and elusive world.

The collection also includes a love sequence, snapshots recalling New York and Florida, a nostalgic look back to Henderson's boyhood in Liverpool, and some of his most popular performance poems.

'The best poems are very good indeed, dangerously good,' Nigel Forde.

Liverpool-born poet and writer Stewart Henderson performs his work all over the UK and abroad. He is the author of *Assembled in Britain* and *Homeland* and is featured in several anthologies.